GERMANY IN THE GREAT WAR

The Opening Year

Mobilisation, the Advance & Naval Warfare

Joshua Bilton

Pen & Sword
MILITARY

First published in Great Britain in 2017 by
PEN & SWORD MILITARY
an imprint of
Pen & Sword Books Ltd,
47 Church Street, Barnsley,
South Yorkshire.
S70 2AS

ISBN 978 1 47382 7 424

A CIP catalogue record for this book is available
from the British Library

Printed and bound in England
By CPI Group (UK) Ltd, Croydon, CR0 4YY

Pen & Sword Books Ltd incorporates the imprints of
Pen & Sword Aviation, Pen & Sword Maritime,
Pen & Sword Military, Pen & Sword Select, Pen & Sword Military Classics,
Leo Cooper, Wharncliffe Local History

For a complete list of Pen & Sword titles please contact:
PEN & SWORD BOOKS LIMITED
47 Church Street, Barnsley, South Yorkshire, S70 2AS, England.
E-mail: enquiries@pen-and-sword.co.uk
Website: www.pen-and-sword.co.uk

Contents

Acknowledgements

There are two people I would like to thank for making this book possible: David Bilton and Anne Coulson, thank you. Any mistakes or omissions on the part of the author are accidental and should be treated as such.

Introduction

'If, as history and nature teaches us, final victory does indeed always go to the good, the just, the progressive, then in this immense, fiery struggle the holy German cause will eventually win out.'

(Verhey, 2000, p.118, quoting from *Kösliner Zeitung* 11 August 1914)

In writing a book that documents the build-up of all German forces in the lead up to and during the first year of the Great War, it is necessary to consider and understand the extent to which the newly created German Empire had expanded by the eve of war. Unlike France and Russia, which by the end of 1914 were fighting a static, stalemated campaign in Europe, Germany faced a war spread over six theatres of operation. With a navy, the rival of Great Britain, fighting around the globe, with military operations in the Far East, in East, West and South West Africa and on three separate fronts in Europe, Germany was not only fighting a static war of attrition, but also engaging in a conflict that varied according to the zone of action and operation, dictated by climate, geography, politics and even language. Deeply committed to all of these theatres of war, Germany dispatched expeditionary forces to remote and distant locations: the Middle East, Macedonia, the Northern Italian peninsular, as well as advisors to the Ottoman army and navy. The German Empire had been forged in the crucible of war and war was its most profitable enterprise.

Following Germany in her struggle were the countries known simply as the Central Powers: Austria-Hungary, in November 1914 Turkey (the Ottoman Empire) and Bulgaria, or the Kingdom of Bulgaria, which entered the war mid-October 1915 (Italy had a defensive alliance with the Central Powers but instead opted to fight with the Allies, eager to obtain Austria's Italian speaking territories). Together with this 'band of brothers' there was a clutch of various dependent colonies and territories of the Central Powers.

The German Empire by 1914 stretched from Klaipeda, Lithuania in the east, to the borders of France, Belgium and Luxembourg in the west. German overseas colonies numbered some sixteen separate protectorates. Military expenditure had seen an increase – a parallel to the growth of colonial possessions – from $398,000,000 dollars in 1908 to $572,000,000 in 1913, an annual rise of $29,000,000 dollars. By the advent of war in just over 40 years, the German Empire had emerged; it was no longer a loose federation of independent states, nor a second-rate, second-place economic, military and colonial competitor of the western European powers, Germany was now a united Fatherland, its history marked by aggression – but also with massive economic development and social innovation. Germany dominated the newspaper headlines, prior to and in consequence of 1914. A myriad of tactical and strategically planned military manoeuvres transformed Europe. In the five months of war of 1914, Germany suffered 800,000 casualties, Austria 1,270,000 killed or wounded at the hands of the Serbs and Russians, and the French 850,000. In the city of Louvain in Belgium, roughly 300,000 medieval books and manuscripts were deliberately burned and approximately 2,000 buildings destroyed.

1914 represented in effect 'a perfect storm' of conflicting interests. An accumulative association of many factors resulted in the outbreak of war and the devastation of much of a continent – physically and emotionally – in less than five months. Winston Churchill wrote afterwards: 'No part of the Great War compares in interest with its opening.' Television's Edmund Blackadder suggested, with more than a hint of truth, that 'the real reason for the whole thing was that it was too much effort not to have a war.'

Chapter One:
Mobilisierung – Österreich und Deutschland
(Mobilization – Austria and Germany)

'Imperial Germany can be said to date from 18 January 1871, when King William I of Prussia was proclaimed Emperor. It is not, however, as simple to determine an exact date for the formation of the German National Army.'

(Bavarian military plenipotentiary Hugo Graf von und zu Lerchenfeld writing to Bavarian *Minister-präsident* Georg Freiherr von Hertling. Quoted in Nash, 1980, p.13)

In 1864, Prussia began an extended campaign (1864-71) whose ultimate goal was unification of all the German states, with the deliberation exception of Austria. Less than fifteen years previously, Prussian military mobilization, 'a well-oiled machine by 1914' (Woodward, 1978), had been ineffectual and dangerously slow. Mobilization during the Olmütz crisis of 1850 took a staggering six weeks to complete. Reservists, recently discharged, reported to their stations late, with little or no recent training and lacking both uniform and equipment. The soldiers therefore fought whilst equipped with an array of antiquated weaponry and associated equipment.

Helmuth Karl Bernhard Graf von Moltke was appointed Chief of the Prussian General Staff in 1857, a position he was to hold for the next thirty years. Taking what historian David Woodward described as an army displaying 'a lack-luster [sic] spirit' (Woodward, 1978), Moltke proceeded to overhaul the strategic purpose, as well as the organization and training of the military. By embracing both the upper and lower echelons of Prussian military society, he was able to reorganize the core hierarchical infrastructure that had dominated Prussian military rule for centuries.

By 1900 the peacetime establishment of the army was set at 545,000 – considerably smaller than that of France or Russia. However, the number of enrolled men for war was set at 6,213,000 comprising an offensive force of 3,013,000 and a *Landsturm* of 3,200,000. This meant that, in the autumn of 1914, Germany was able to mobilize eighty-seven divisions, while the French had a mere sixty-two.

On 2 August 1914, the first day of mobilization, the German ranks were filled to wartime capacity with the most recently discharged reservists. With the ranks filled and the soldiers accounted for, entire regiments marched out of their depots, leaving behind a small number of specialist staff: cadres, medical personnel and the administrative section. Quickly the barracks were again filled: this time with reserve troops. Clothed and equipped, these formations were organized into reserve units and shipped to the appropriate theatre of war, following the movements of the regular army. In the rush following the announcement of war, many regimental commanders found discrepancies in the number of men under their command. Some were under strength, while others found themselves with an abundance of manpower. Despite inconsistencies, German mobilization was an unparalleled success. During the first six days alone, the peacetime army of 840,000 would swell to 3,840,000 and 'field armies containing 2,100,000 soldiers were deployed on the Eastern and Western Fronts.'

On 30 July 1914, the Austro-Hungarian General Staff issued orders for the general mobilization of all Austrian forces, three days in advance of their German allies. At the time of mobilization, Austria and Hungary each had a separate peacetime standing army. It was these combined armies of the Austro-Hungarian Empire that went 'into the field for the Great War of 1914'. They 'were the heirs and successors of men who had defeated the Turks at Vienna [and] given Napoleon's forces their first European setback.'

The mobilization of Austrian forces in the autumn of 1914 resulted in a total of 102 Austro-Hungarian infantry regiments (Nr.1-102) and four regiments of the Bosnian-Herzegovinian Army (Nr.1-4). Each of the 106 regiments to enter the field that autumn was divided into four battalions, each one of which consisted of four companies with an additional replacement cadre staff (Ersatzkader) and subsequent machine gun detachment per battalion.

On the eve of war, the combined Austro-Hungarian peacetime strength amounted to 350,000 men. With mobilization came a three-fold increase in those numbers, giving a total of forty-nine available infantry divisions. Of the 3,350,000 officers and men to enter service, only 1,421,000 saw frontline action in the next four years. Of those 3,350,000 troops, 28 percent were native Austrian/German, 44 percent (nearly half) were Slavs, 18 percent Hungarian, with the remaining Roumanian and Italian peoples of the Empire respectively contributing just 8 and 2 percent.

As news of the assassination at Sarajevo reached the troops stationed at home, tensions rose and throngs of truculent, militaristic reservists engulfed the streets, pavements and railway stations, many marching in organized bodies on their way to report for duty. Inside many barracks chaos reigned: a breakdown in communication meant that the influx of military reservists could not be handled. The men slept on the floor, eating what and when they could. Such chaos was not total. Some depots found that they were able to absorb not only discharged reservists, but also thousands of volunteers who came forward to serve their country. Both Germany and Austria-Hungary had now mobilized for war, a war that was to last far beyond Christmas 1914, the date by which many over sanguine people thought that the war would be won.

GWG14_1. The shadow of despair: Prince Lichnowsky, German Ambassador to the Court of St James's, walking in St James' Park having been informed by the Foreign Office of the British ultimatum to Germany.

GWG14_3. A German airship in the course of construction. Below the frame of the dirigible lies the exterior fabric lining of the airship.

GWG14_4. A German siege gun.

GWG14_2. German infantry bound for the front, march in formation with loved ones and friends alongside.

GWG14_9. German infantry recruits lie prone, awaiting the order 'Attack', part of a training exercise.

GWG14_5. German cavalry take up position during pre-war manoeuvres.

GWG14_6. An officer of the 1st Prussian Foot Guards in field uniform.

GWG14_15. A trooper of the Death's Head Hussars smiles for the camera.

GWG14_8. An officer of the 1st Prussian Foot Guards in parade uniform poses for the camera in a photographer's studio.

GWG14_87 Newly enlisted recruits of the Guards are sworn in at Potsdam before the Kaiser.

GWG14_16. Field Marshal Wilhelm Leopold Colmar Freiherr von der Goltz, appointed military governor of Belgium for a brief period, dealt harshly with all acts of Belgian sabotage and resistance.

GWG14_17. General Alexander Heinrich Rudolph von Kluck, commander of the First Army.

GWG14_10. A German armoured car, equipped with a Krupp siege cannon installed at rear is its rear, is set up for the anti-aircraft defence role.

GWG14_11. Firing position: a revealing shot of a German armoured car, mounting a Krupp cannon showing clearly the layout of the vehicle. A hatch at the rear of the vehicle allows the gunner to operate the weapon, while a compartment behind the driver accommodates the cartridge cases and shells of the gun. These were designed to deal with the new threat to military operations – aircraft.

GWG14_14. General (promoted to Field Marshal in January 1915) Wilhelm Paul von Bülow, who commanded the Second Army. Controversially, he was appointed senior to von Kluck, commanding First Army. Concerned by the growing gap between the two armies, in early September von Kluck was tasked with closing the gap, thus ensuring that the Germans did not envelop Paris but passed to its east, enabling the French and British armies to carry out a counter stroke on the Marne.

GWG14_19. Rupprecht, Crown Prince of Bavaria; commander Sixth Army.

GWG14_13. A section of German artillerymen using a haystack for cover. An observer, far left, is assessing the range of potential targets. The men kneeling (third from right) and standing (far right) are laying a telephone cable – note the reels of cable held by each man.

GWG14_20. Crowds in Berlin cheer the declaration of war.

GWG14_18. Wilhelm, Crown Prince of Germany, resplendent in the uniform of the Death's Head Hussars; he was titular commander of Fifth Army.

GWG14_12. German gunners observing for targets note the bulbous, rather than pointed, finial (spike) atop the *pickelhaube*, standard for the German artillery.

GWG14_21. The declaration of war in Berlin: an enthusiastic crowd gathers in front of the Royal Palace, awaiting the Imperial appearance on the balcony and a speech justifying the war.

GWG14_25. An assorted array of captured enemy artillery passes through the Brandenburg Gate in Berlin. This illustration is reproduced from a picture-postcard called a *kriegskarte*, or war-card. The caption translates: 'The first signs of victory in Berlin. Bringing in captured Russian, Belgian and French guns through the Brandenburg Gate'.

GWG14_24. Count Zeppelin – seated far right, creator and namesake of the dirigible airship, Zeppelin – attending manoeuvres held in 1913, in discussion with the Kaiser (standing, far left).

GWG14_23. Gustav Steinhauer, the Kaiser's master spy and officer of the Imperial German Navy was, from 1901, the head of the British section of the German Admiralty's intelligence service the *Nachrichten-Abteilung*. 'N'. He established a spy network in Britain before the war.

GWG14_28. A thanksgiving service for victory: citizens of Berlin gather as part of a religious ceremony in front of the Bismarck memorial, which was moved to the Tiergarten by order of Hitler in 1938.

GWG14_27. Crown Prince Rupprecht of Bavaria, seated far right, plots his next move in the splendour of a 'liberated' French châteaux.

GWG14_26. German Reservists of the (Prussian Guard) Infanterie-Regiment Nr. 4 departing from the city of Potsdam. Graffiti on a carriage car reads 'Express to Paris'.

GWG14_36. A search dog of the Red Cross works independently of his handler and finds a 'casualty'.

GWG14_37. German medical orderlies with their working dog, his medical mission clearly indicated and equipped for field service with a flask and a carrying case, containing an assortment of medical supplies.

GWG14_38. A class of trainees, civilian handlers and Red Cross dogs, observe a demonstration enacted by two experienced members of the German medical branch.

GWG14_35. Training in the field: a dog leads a civilian tracker to where a 'wounded' soldier lies prone amidst the foliage of a woodland area.

GWG14_22. An 11-inch German siege mortar, sitting on its specialist limber, moves towards the front line.

GWG14_32. Germany's answer to Kitchener's army: war volunteers (*Kriegsfreiwilligen*). Just as British volunteers posed for newspaper photographers on their training grounds, so do this German section – but they seem to be better equipped.

GWG14_33. An adapted truck converted to enable it to transport a field gun – in this photograph a 7.7cm Feldkanone 96 (7.7cm FK 96). It used two grooved rails to ensure that it was loaded into the appropriate position on the truck bed.

GWG14_31. Each sporting a fine set of whiskers, these three men from the East Frisian Islands have their photograph taken for posterity before heading off to war.

GWG14_34. The 7.7cm Feldkanone 96 pictured on the truck. It is secured in its position by folding the tracks over the wheels and connecting them to the bars to the rear of the cab. It is not likely that this arrangement would have been particularly practical, especially when the war settled down into the stalemate of trench warfare.

GWG14_30. The interior of 'Cannon-Workshop No.5' in Essen, a huge working space in which the finishes were applied to artillery pieces.

GWG14_29. A specially constructed Krupp railway wagon, designed to transport the heavier of the range of Krupp artillery pieces.

Chapter Two:
Vormarsch nach Westen (Western Advance)

'Germany cannot respect Belgium's neutrality [...] an offensive war [*Angriffskrieg*]
against France would only be possible along the lines of Belgium.' (Ehlert *et al*.
2014, p.49)

In 1914 the German Army 'was irrevocably committed to a strategy of offence. Victorious campaigns, it was argued, could only be achieved by vigorous offensive action.' According to Field Marshal Graf Alfred von Schlieffen's famous memorandum composed on the eve of retirement in 1905, the war against France was supposed to be 'a quick victory,' a precursor to the invasion of Russia. To this end, almost the entire weight of the German Army was employed to the Western Front with a large percentage of its manpower involved in the advance through neutral Belgium. It is arguable that France may have been defeated in 1914 had the German offensive attained wide-ranging success in enveloping all French military forces, and 'had not Moltke evinced a considerable display of indecision, verging on panic, in the first weeks of the war'.

On 2 August, a company of 69 Infantry Regiment, commanded by Lieutenant Feldmann, crossed the border with Luxembourg; the following day Fourth Army occupied the country. German troops entered Belgium on 4 August, but Second Army faced an unexpectedly lengthy siege of Liège, which lasted over ten days. First Army meanwhile advanced toward Tongres and Antwerp. The Belgian Government, wary of the swift advance, abandoned Brussels on 17 August. France fought a series of hugely expensive battles on its eastern frontier with Germany and then was compelled to withdraw, whilst Joffre, the commander in chief, prepared to counter the Germans on the left by redeploying a significant part of his field army. Belgian resistance centred on Antwerp. At the Battle of Mons, on 23 and 24 August, the First Army encountered the four infantry divisions and a cavalry division of the British Expeditionary Force (BEF). The British force retired and there began the Retreat from Mons, which did not end until 5 September. On 25 August 'one million Germans invaded France' as troops poured over the Franco-Belgian border. Five of the seven German armies 'scythed down towards Paris on a 75-mile front', largely unopposed. Maintaining the advance, First Army, commanded by General von Kluck, attacked the retreating British II Corps west of Le Cateau. In a somewhat confused battle, II Corps was able to withdraw after suffering substantial losses – between 5,000 and 7,500 men, a significant number of whom were prisoners, and twenty-five guns. The Germans suffered fewer casualties – since they owned the battlefield at the end of the day, they lost very few men as prisoners. However, instead of pursuing the British, the Germans loitered for a vital 24 hours: whilst von Kluck made the error of thinking that the British were heading south west, whereas they were heading south.

Despite inflicting substantial losses, it was obvious that all was not going well with the German attack. The decision by Bulow to order von Kluck's First Army to close up with his Second Army led to the fateful decision to turn First Army south eastwards and therefore passing to the east of Paris rather than the west. Joffre's brilliant improvisation meant that the allies were able to launch a counterattack at the Marne on 6 September and by the 9th, the First and Second Armies fell back. In the southeast, at the Battle of Grand Couronné (4–12 September), the German Sixth Army narrowly failed in its attempt to take Nancy. The Kaiser was briefly in attendance, having travelled down from Berlin in order to supervise the attack and seizure of the city.

The situation after the Marne was stabilised at the Battle of the Aisne (12–15 September) and it is from this point that many consider that trench warfare began. What then followed was a series of attempts to outflank the northern edge of the two opposing armies, sometimes misleadingly known as the Race to the Sea, which culminated in the frantic fighting between Ypres and the coast, involving Belgian, French and British troops against the desperate efforts of the Germans to break through: the battle officially ended on 22 November.

From 28 September to 7 October, German forces besieged Antwerp. The outlying ring of forts, (forty-eight in total) was shelled continually by German siege artillery, including the use of the powerful 'Big Bertha' guns. Four German divisions, comprising mainly reserve troops, succeeded in penetrating two of the outer forts on 2 October. The order to evacuate was given and the city occupied by nightfall on 7 October. The bulk of the Belgian field army and the British 7th Division managed to make good their escape; the remaining Belgian forces formally surrendered on 10 October.

The last major action on the Western Front in 1914, the First Battle of Champagne, began on 20 December and did not officially come to a close until 17 March 1915. By the end of the year, the war of mobility on this front had come to an end, stalled by winter, exhaustion, and a truly alarming expenditure of war materiel. It was not to return until the spring of 1918. For now, the defence, ensconced in increasingly complicated trench systems, supported by artillery and the awesome effectiveness of machine guns, was dominant: that situation became the norm for 'Der Westfront im Erste Weltkrieg'.

GWG14_40. The Avenue de Maastricht, Visé, following the German advance: the photograph indicates something of the grim reality and horror of war.

GWG14_39. The occupation of Brussels: German infantry occupy the Court of Appeal, one of several courts making up the Palace of Justice (this magnificent building, bigger than St Peter's Basilica in Rome, often accommodated up to 10,000 men).

GWG14_42.2. Kaiser Wilhelm in discussion with the Bavarian Crown Prince during a parade in the field.

GWG14_41. Members of the (6th West Prussian) Infanterie-Regiment Nr. 149 (regimental numbers were sewn or stenciled in green on the front of the M1892 Überzug – helmet cover) search the rubble of a fire-damaged house in Visé.

GWG14_47. A group of arrested Belgians, suspected of being *franc-tireus* (irregular combatants not in uniform), await their fate. Military justice tended to be superficial, especially in these early months of the war.

GWG14_45. A Belgian peasant, suspected of espionage, is interrogated under the watchful gaze of some Prussian infantrymen.

GWG14_44. A German Infanterie-Regiment marches through the Place Charles Rogier, passing in front of crowds of Belgians who are braving a heavy downpour to witness the scene.

GWG14_42. German troops make the most of a midday break during their march 'Nach Paris'.

GWG14_52. Prince Rupprecht of Bavaria, using his hand to emphasize a point, in earnest discussion with the Kaiser.

GWG14_46. Belgian civilians are ordered to turn out their pockets; the Germans enforced strict measures on the local population of newly conquered territory.

GWG14_49. German cavalry trot past the royal palace in Brussels in review order.

GWG14_50. Christmas 1914: belligerents on both sides in a number of places engaged in an informal truce. British and German infantry are shown in this artist's impression, fraternizing, having their photograph taken whilst enjoying some Christmas cheer.

GWG14_48. German cavalry often moved well in advance of the main body; here some stop to water their horses at a Belgian village trough.

GWG14_43. Uhlans use dogs to help pull a cartload of supplies. The Belgians, in particular, made a lot of use of dogs to pull smaller carts.

GWG14_53. A German encampment on the outskirts of Ostend, Belgium.

GWG14_55. A Belgian town becomes the scene of German military activity; something that would become the norm for the next four years.

GWG14_56. A local man is interrogated whilst on his journey home by a patrol of German soldiers outside Brussels.

GWG14_51. German infantry erect temporary stabling on the outlying fringes of a dense wood, possibly Houthulst Forest, in northern Belgium.

GWG14_54. News from the front: several German soldiers make use of a quiet moment to get letters written. The postal services of all armies were extraordinarily efficient.

GWG14_62. Two signallers repair a fractured telephone cable.

GWG14_61. Wheat requestioned by the Germans is prepared for distribution.

GWG14_59. German officers superintend a soldier – firing from a raised platform, a table top – during target practice.

GWG14_71. In a trench beyond the Yser, German infantry prepare their ammunition clips.

GWG14_57. Operating along the coast: a German naval machine gun section stands guard on the Channel coast.

GWG14_58. An observation balloon is filled with gas, with the supply concealed in a nearby haystack.

GWG14_65. A German observation post hidden from observation by a stack of hay; his periscope has been camouflaged by using straw.

GWG14_64. Belgian prisoners – or civilians – are set to work digging trenches under German guard.

GWG14_66. A very informal pay parade: German infantry collect their pay (in notes) from a *Feldwebel* (Warrant Officer) while serving at the front.

GWG14_63. A German soldier enjoys the facilities of his earthen 'hotel suite'.

GWG14_73. A relaxed scene in a crowded German trench. There appears to be only one man keeping an eye on the enemy, whilst the rest read, smoke and sleep. Note the straw at the bottom of the trench, which is beginning to develop a permanent look.

GWG14_60. Facing ground that had been deliberately inundated by the Belgians, German infantry, in a primitive trench, look over the Yser. A range finder has been placed on the parapet.

GWG14_67. German marines aboard a train that the chalked notice on a carriage states is bound for Calais-Dover – somewhat prematurely, as neither place was reached by the Germans.

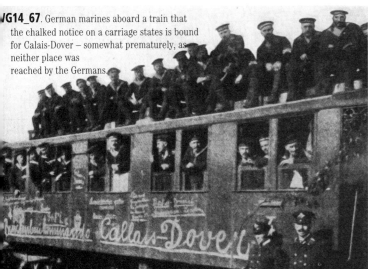

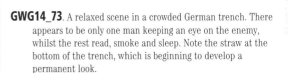

GWG14_76. By the close of 1914 the Belgian army was reduced to holding a small part of the coast around Furnes/Veurne. German marines set about establishing complex defences of their conquered coast line.

GWG14_74. German infantry, well protected from fire beneath a concrete roof shelter.

GWG14_75. Marines manning a Maxim MG08, positioned on a sand dune. The *Marines-Korps-Flandern* (Marine [or Naval] Corps Flanders) fought at the extreme north of the line.

GWG14_70. German infantry rejoice in the capture of a 120mm L de Bange Modele 1878 gun. The gun was, in reality, old and almost obsolete – the barrel was fine, but it was exceptionally slow to reload.

GWG14_77. Admiral von Schröder (centre, with sword), with his staff and army officers in the town of Dixmuid after its fall in November 1914. He commanded the Naval Corps Flanders throughout the war.

GWG14_80. The mounting of an Austrian Skoda siege mortar – the 30.5cm (305mm/12-inch) Belagerungsmorser – being transported to a new location.

GWG14_81. A German court of inquiry investigates the case of a peasant accused of aiding his fellow countrymen escape from occupied Belgium; the first witness is his son.

GWG14_72. German riflemen take cover behind a makeshift barricade, engaged in one of the numerous skirmishes of the early months of the war.

GWG14_84. German prisoners en route to a prisoner of war camp pass through a cordon of British soldiers, whilst a mixed group of soldiers and civilians look on.

GWG14_79. On loan from Austria: a massive 30.5cm (305mm/12-inch) *Belagerungsmorser* mortar, manufactured by Skoda, and its team. The weapon was very effective in reducing Belgium's 'impregnable' fortresses, such as those of Namur and Liège.

GWG14_68. A London motor omnibus: captured at the fall of Antwerp, it is now being used to transport German troops and their kit.

GWG14_78. The occupiers make use of an adapted Ostend tram (two freight wagons have been attached to the rear) to transport men and equipment. Men of the 5th Marines, including at least one complete machine gun team.

GWG14_85. *Nach Paris*: 'Free trip via Liège to Paris', is written across a cattle carriage door. German infantry, eager to come to grips with the French, on their way to the front.

GWG14_69. German infantry and cavalry in the shadow of a burnt out church, symbolic of the destruction of war.

GWG14_88. A German 7.7cm FK 96 field gun camouflaged by a mass of vegetation: a precaution against enemy observers.

GWG14_83. A propaganda picture of a bathing party: British prisoners, each given a towel, formed up for a bath.

GWG14_94. Relaxed German prisoners shod with Belgian sabots. The original caption said that the poor quality of German boots had cut the men's feet to pieces. They are under Belgian guard in the city of Bruges.

GWG14_82. Victorious German cavalry move through Louvain against the backdrop of its charred buildings. The willful destruction of Louvain by the Germans was a propaganda disaster.

GWG14_87. German troops pose for a photograph amidst the ruins of a Belgian casement; the officer at the front is a doctor.

GWG14_93. German cavalry officers, wounded during the advance on Liège, receive medical attention from a medical orderly beside a temporary straw shelter.

GWG14_92. German troops are issued a hot meal in the Grande Place, Brussels.

GWG14_96. Field-Marshal von der Goltz, appointed military governor of Belgium on 26 August. Because of his extensive service with the Ottomans between 1883 and 1895, he was appointed military aide to the Sultan in October 1914.

GWG14_86. German supply wagons move through a deserted street in the damaged village of Mouland. Notice in the background smoke rising from several houses, almost certainly deliberately set ablaze.

GWG14_91. German infantry at rest following an intense period of heavy fighting at Visé.

GWG14_98. A cavalcade of infantry and artillery move through the streets of Brussels.

GWG14_103. A German patrol on the beach at Ostend.

GWG14_97. German infantry march at ease along a flower-lined street in the city of Brussels.

GWG14_95. The scene at a German encampment established after the action at Visé. Belgian prisoners are gathered in the hollow on the left, whilst in the foreground a group of Belgian spectators look on.

GWG14_89. A review of troops in the shattered remnants of Louvain.

GWG14_90. A detachment of German sentries on the bank of the River Meuse. Only one of them stands guard, the remainder enjoying a very relaxing time.

GWG14_99. On the march to Brussels: German soldiers are served a ration of ham and bread.

GWG14_102. 'A great light projector' (i.e. a searchlight) is towed by trucks towards the front. Part of a heavy gun detachment, Austrian officers are seated in the car whilst the men are relegated to bench seating on the truck.

GWG14_104. An artillery observation party takes advantage of the lie of the land for cover to examine the enemy's dispositions.

GWG14_101. A concentration of German machine guns, along with some medical wagons, are drawn up in suburban Brussels awaiting an order to move.

GWG14_108. German infantry, being transported by rail from Malines, find their progress halted by the wreckage of several locomotives and carriages that have very effectively blocked the line.

GWG14_100. German 28cm Krupp siege mortar.

GWG14_110. The Uhlan who, it is claimed, got 'nearest to England'. He was awarded the Iron Cross, the story goes, for going alone ahead of a patrol to scout, and made his way to the forward-most fringe of the enemy line.

GWG14_105. German sailors on the quay at Antwerp guard equipment and materiel abandoned by the Belgian and British defenders – a potent symbol of defeated troops.

GWG14_111. The fall of Antwerp: a street adjacent to the cathedral, congested by an array of motorcars laden with panic-stricken refugees endeavoring to escape the city.

GWG14_109. Two German soldiers stand on top of a steel reinforced cupola, part of the Maubeuge fortifications destroyed by a German shell.

GWG14_114. A German naval cadet armed with a vicious looking saw-edge bayonet on his rifle. With his other hand he plants a flag on a captured Belgian army position.

GWG14_116. German Landsturm – distinguished by their obsolete shakos, issued because of a shortage of standard caps – construct an effigy of a Belgian refugee as a target.

GWG14_106. German sailors of the naval brigade enter Antwerp following the evacuation of the city by the allies. These seamen were drawn from members of the High Seas Fleet and were dispatched to supplement the army in the field, releasing soldiers for the fighting to the west.

GWG14_107. Early German occupiers of Ghent; several of them, including some cyclists, confer with civic authorities.

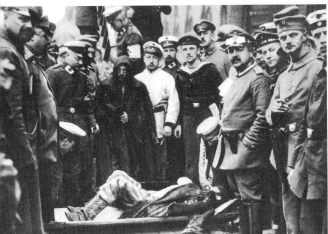

GWG14_115. Wounded Belgian soldiers are used for a photo-opportunity. The one on a stretcher has just been lifted out from an ambulance by medical orderlies; the other stands in the centre, hooded and looking utterly miserable, surrounded by a cluster of German infantry and sailors.

GWG14_112. Male inhabitants of the 'late city of Louvain' are escorted into Brussels.

GWG14_120. A concealed German gun crew stands prepared for action: though the effect is somewhat spoiled by the prominent position of the gun commander.

GWG14_117. Belgian men on their way to dig a succession of military entrenchments, preparatory to an expected German attack.

GWG14_119. A treacherous tract of French marshland is crossed by a 546-yard long elevated road constructed by German engineers, a task that took five days and employed 600 men.

GWG14_113. German cowherds: armed German marines muster a herd of Belgian cattle, commandeered to supplement their basic supplies.

GWG14_118. German marines develop a gun pit for what appears to be a 7.7cm Feldkanone 96 (7.7cm FK 96) field gun, as part of the defences near Ostend.

GWG14_122. German soldiers celebrate the arrival of Christmas and the long awaited presents that this will bring.

GWG14_123a. A group of Bavarian infantry officers chat with each other in a quiet location on the line in the mountainous and wooded Vosges.

GWG14_121. German motorboat with a for'ard mounted Maxim MG08 machine gun, covers a stretch of the river at Ostend.

GWG14_124. Men of the Bavarian *Landsturm* stand to attention; their only consistent piece of military equipment, is the 7.92mm M 98 (Gewehr 98) rifle.

GWG14_129. The ruins of a French estaminet (a small café that also sold alcohol) destroyed by German shelling – retribution for the 'loss' of a chair.

GWG14_128. Fraternisation at Christmas: German and British soldiers exchange greetings in front of their trenches in No Man's Land.

GWG14_123. Preparatory to a winter campaign, canal barges laden with sleighs are being ferried for the use of Alpine troops fighting in the Vosges Mountains, Alsace-Lorraine.

GWG14_130. 'Music hath charms to soothe the savage breast': a company of German infantry enjoys a prolonged halt, enjoying – or possibly not, judging by some of the expressions – the playing of a melodeon.

GWG14_127. A German military choir: German infantry sing carols on the dunes at the northern extremity of the *Westfront*. One wonders what the sole sentry is looking for, given the general air of relaxation.

GWG14_125. A travelling field kitchen serves a hot dinner during the midday halt.

GWG14_126. A captured field gun is paraded through the streets of Stuttgart.

GWG14_136. 'The mounted vandals of the Kaiser', says the original caption: a cavalry camp close to the Belgian border. Along the length of the closest horse line is a line of helmets (*pickelhaube*), perched on top of cavalry swords and rifles.

GWG14_138. Midday ration: ham and bread is served to German infantry during their advance towards Brussels.

GWG14_133. Thirsty German soldiers near Visé: a limited ration of water – though judging by the looks on their faces it might be something more exciting – is distributed amongst a troop of German infantry billeted in the residential district of Moelingen (Mouland).

GWG14_137. German infantry take advantage of a pause in fighting after victory at Visé and take the weight off their feet. They await the order to continue the advance.

GWG14_135. German cavalry – hussars – cross the Meuse in canvas boats bound together by their lances.

GWG14_140. The flower of the German army: Hussar officers – sent in to impress the people of Brussels – study Belgian newspapers on the Chaussée de Louvain.

GWG14_134. Forage wagons pass through the town of Mouland, one of the first to be torched by the First Army in its advance westwards from the border city of Aix la Chapelle (Aachen).

GWG14_144. Infantry of IX Reserve Corps, commanded by General von Boehn, on the march in Flanders.

GWG14_145. One of the weaknesses of the Schlieffen Plan lay in the great physical demands it made on the troops, particularly the infantry, who more often than not had to march everywhere; they naturally took any opportunity to grab some rest.

GWG14_139. German troops requisition transport and supplies in their march westwards.

GWG14_147. Marines of a German *Seebataillon* pose with their machine guns in a wood in Belgium. They must have had a very restricted field of fire. The marine standing at the right is a bicycle messenger.

GWG14_132. German soldiers billeted in a Belgian village fill their leather water containers from a Belgian farmer's well and pump; the water pail was carried round the ranks twice daily.

GWG14_131. A column of German infantry and cyclists marches toward an unknown objective.

GWG14_141. Members of the Guards Corps off duty in the Belgian capital.

GWG14_142. The German military governor of Brussels, General von Lüttwitz, riding through the streets of Brussels.

GWG14_143. Notifications – military proclamations – posted outside the Hotel de Ville attract their usual morning crowd.

GWG14_146. German hussars blocking the Chaussée de Louvain, Brussels. Notice how much kit the horses are carrying.

GWG14_149. German soldiers relax outside a café whilst a Belgian priest, wearing a Red Cross armband, walks by,

GWG14_148. German soldiers take advantage of the Burgomaster's garden at Visé and furniture that has, presumably, been removed from his house, to set about preparing a meal.

GWG14_150. German infantry distribute a meagre daily allowance of food to the hungry inhabitants, mainly children, of Bruges. The German seizure of foodstuffs left residents short, something that was not going to get better during the war years.

GWG14_153. Belgians accused of being franc-tireurs – combatants in civilian garb – stand in a line by a family home in Belgium, awaiting their fate, all too often execution by firing squad.

GWG14_154. German troops lie spread across verge and pavement. Scenes such as this were commonplace in the summer of 1914 in the sprawling suburbs of Brussels.

GWG14_152. Three women, residents of a home in Termonde, refuse to abandon their home in the light of the threat of shelling but sensibly have moved down to the basement floor.

GWG14_151. The body of a Belgian peasant killed by a German shell lies in rubble while a boy stares at the pitiful scene.

GWG14_156. The Palais de Justice, Brussels: the centre of the German military government is suitably protected by sentries, sandbags and artillery.

GWG14_155. A German artillery piece near to the Palais de Justice is positioned for rapid use, part of the policy of overawing the population with a display of military might.

GWG14_157. A prepared defensive position located behind the Palais de Justice, Brussels. The low level wall has been strengthened by the addition of sandbags.

GWG14_159. Dinner parade: German infantry, mess tins at the ready, muster in the barracks square at Mons, eagerly anticipating their midday meal.

GWG14_160. Bringing German *kultur* to Dinant: the German commandant, Obersleutnant Beeger (seated rear left), and a German professor (rear right), set off to inspect the town as part of a plan to overhaul the school curriculum.

GWG14_163. A German field artillery piece and its team makes a temporary halt.

GWG14_161. An officer's patrol moves ahead of the main body to check the ground and identify any enemy troops.

GWG14_164. Lieutenant von Bismarck, an ordnance officer, in discussion with a despatch rider somewhere in the Flanders region.

GWG14_162. Infantry and cyclists of a German Landwehr regiment advance across terrain deliberately flooded by the Belgians in the area of the Yser, making their way towards the front line.

GWG14_167. A German chaplain reads the service from his prayer book at the well attended burial of a soldier killed in Belgium.

GWG14_166. German marines guard a bridge on the approach to Ostend from Bruges.

GWG14_165. German artillery officers testing a French Mle 1914 Hotchkiss machine gun mounted in a cemetery in Diksmuide. The officer at the gun is taking advantage of a handy tomb slab as a seat.

GWG14_169. On guard at the Dutch frontier: German soldiers (left) stand under a German flag attached to a pylon; whilst Dutch sentries stand next to their rudimentary sentry box. No one seems to be taking much interest in the train.

GWG14_158. An imaginative use of a haystack has provided this sentry with a billet – and he has added to his comfort with a board on which to stand.

GWG14_174. German cavalry wade across a river in France.

GWG14_170. German marines carry the luggage of Belgian refugees coerced into returning to the German occupied city of Antwerp.

GWG14_173. The bodies of French cavalry horses are strewn across a street in Lille. Cavalry was probably at its least effective in a built up area and would have made easy targets for German troops.

GWG14_168. German gunners manhandle a field gun into position at Antwerp in anticipation of a Belgian counter attack.

GWG14_177. German officers and a sergeant major sit in conference discussing orders for the following day over a couple of bottles of wine that were probably 'liberated' from a Belgian café cellar. The wagon behind them is for transporting forage.

GWG14_176. A fortified farmhouse: a rear guard detachment of German machine gunners await the advance of French forces.

GWG14_179. Access to fresh or drinkable water was a major problem for all sides: here a German mobile water purification unit is setting about its vital task.

GWG14_175. Sinister 'birds' make their nest in the roof: German machine gunners make u of a French farmhouse as a makeshift blockhouse with a good field of fire.

GWG14_178. Tired German infantry welcome a lift in a farmer's cart as they follow up the retreating allies. The distances that the armies had to walk in the summer and autumn of 1914 were very great and many of the soldiers were wearing in brand new boots.

GWG14_172. German occupation of Lille: with an attempt at street decoration the Crown Prince of Bavaria (central figure, mounted) makes his formal entrance into Lille at the head of his army, in tribute to the Crown Prince.

GWG14_180. Medical orderlies heading towards the front, led by an NCO who has the ribbon of the Iron Cross, second class, in his tunic buttonhole. They are likely battalion stretcher bearers, as they are carrying rifles.

GWG14_182. Two dismounted Uhlans pose for the camera, manning a shallow trench, somewhere in northern France.

GWG14_184. A much more substantial earthwork – note the sandbags and barbed wire – provides secure shelter for a watchful sentry and an NCO.

GWG14_185. German engineers rebuild a bridge on the outskirts of Kalisch (modern day Kalisz, in Poland), partially demolished by its defenders. Note the pontoon bridge put in place on its left.

GWG14_183. French citizens being removed to the rear in a motley array of farm wagons.

GWG14_181. Signallers establishing communications in northern France.

WG14_186. A British motor ambulance damaged by German shelling; it is open to conjecture as to whether the ambulance got it into the ditch or it was pushed there to get it off the road.

WG14_187. Almost a perfect example of how a trench was supposed to look – a 'castellated' look, which divides the trench into bays and thus some protection against shell blast and enfilade fire; a fire step and straw lining for the floor. Note the shovels and equipment. The trench is still quite shallow and lacks – or appears to lack – any obstacles to its front.

GWG14_189. Wounded German prisoners parade with medical orderlies outside a church at Meaux.

GWG14_191. German infantry manning a defensive position adjoining a French field. An officer to the left of the Maxim MG08 machine gun takes a careful look over No Man's Land.

GWG14_188. A senior German officer awards the Iron Cross to a non-commissioned officer.

GWG14_190. French and German wounded and dying lie abreast in a church near Meaux and under the watchful eye of a French cavalryman.

GWG14_192. A panorama of the western end of the battlefield of the Aisne (12–15 September 1914). The French were on the left and the British line began on the extreme right.

GWG14_194. German infantry defend the north bank of a river from an allied attempt to ford it.

GWG14_196. Many consider that trench warfare began after the Aisne, as both sides settled down into increasingly complex field work defences, such as these early examples of shelters near the river.

GWG14_199. A German 15cm sFH 02 howitzer is manoeuvred into an open firing position – a practice by both sides that was not uncommon at the time. Static warfare generally brought an end to that practice.

GWG14_195. A German cavalry column trots along a muddy, poplar-lined road in northern France.

GWG14_198. Members of a German cavalry regiment water their horses and wash off the sweat in the River Meurthe, having retired from the front, under cover of darkness, the previous evening.

GWG14_193. German trenches guard against a hostile crossing of the River Aisne.

GWG14_202. French and British officers, under guard, march along a road in northern France. The officer on the extreme left of the fore rank is Colonel W.E. Gordon of the Gordon Highlanders, captured at Le Cateau. He won the Victoria Cross during the Boer War for his gallantry in July 1900.

GWG14_200. A well known photograph, possibly pre-war according to some sources. German infantry advance en masse and in extended order across a field of flowers.

GWG14_197. The funeral of a German officer processes through a French village.

GWG14_203. German medics with a Belgian Red Cross dog.

GWG14_201. A German *Unteroffizier* reviews the daily notice on the board on a wall of the regional field post-office.

GWG14_208. German soldiers lie prone in extended order atop a hill in northern France. In the distance, an advancing company of British infantry is visible.

GWG14_209. Weary German infantry move towards the front.

GWG14_205. Whilst some dig trenches under attentive supervision, others put soil into sandbags.

GWG14_206. German infantry escort non combatants before them.

GWG14_207. A medical orderly tends to a wounded German soldier, with a couple of civilians on hand, presumably to help with the removal of the victim.

GWG14_210. Officers of 36th (Magdeburg) Fusiliers 'General Field Marshal Count Blumenthal', pose for the camera.

GWG14_213. Canine ambulance workers: Belgian dogs are employed to assist in recovering the wounded, 'seekers of the wounded'.

GWG14_211. A close formation of German infantry form a skirmish line.

GWG14_212. Two German officers – plus two unidentified recruits – make themselves comfortable in an early trench dugout.

GWG14_214. The first German soldier across the Meuse: officially he clambered 'over a shattered pontoon bridge as it sank under fire from the Liege forts'.

GWG14_217. A solitary Bavarian sentry stands stoically on guard in the snow somewhere in Flanders.

GWG14_218. With the advent of winter, Bavarian sentries in Flanders on outpost duty dress as warmly as possible as they endure glacial winds and heavy snow.

GWG14_219. German infantry carry a French officer to his grave, accompanied by full military honours, including a firing party.

GWG14_216. A German band leads a funeral cortège directed through a French village.

GWG14_223. Like an oversized rabbit warren, these German troops occupy 'burrows' in the Argonne region.

GWG14_221. Makeshift trestle supports are used as temporary anti-aircraft mounts for the Maxim MG08 (Maschinengewehr 08).

GWG14_222. A German artillery observation post: from the comparative safety of a haystack, a German officer transmits his observations to his battery.

GWG14_225. German officers studying a map.

GWG14_224. German soldiers taking advantage of the contents of a café in the town of Mouland.

GWG14_220. A French soldier assists an all but naked German prisoner who was found during the French advance.

GWG14_228. A farmer's plough is used to speed up the cutting of trenches.

GWG14_227. German soldiers digging trenches in northern France. Trench construction was, at this date, still in its infancy, hence the linear rather than traversed nature of the trench.

GWG14_230. Aerial observers receive instruction in the basics of telecommunication.

GWG14_215. An aerial photograph of the fortress town of Longwy reveals the damage caused by German shelling.

GWG14_226. German snipers ready to fire at enemy infantry through loopholes in the walls of a French farmhouse.

GWG14_229. German infantry in action: from a basic trench German soldiers stand alert. Towards the middle of the line of men a range finder is laid horizontally on the parapet.

GWG14_204. British prisoners march in formation, escorted by German infantry, through the village of Döberitz, towards a prisoner of war camp located on the outlying fringes of the village and some twenty miles from Berlin.

GWG14_233. (Top image of two) German *Landsturm* parade before the Crown Prince of Bavaria, following the occupation of Lille.

GWG14_232. German infantry holding the line, making use of a ditch, in the wooded region of the Argonne.

GWG14_238. German artillerymen – two of its members winners of the Iron Cross second class – pose by their gun, camouflaged against enemy observation.

GWG14_239. A group photograph of gunners of the German field artillery

GWG14_235. German infantry pass through a French village on their way to the front line.

GWG14_234. The Bavarian Crown Prince continues his inspection of the German forces at Lille.

GWG14_245. A German field artillery battery behind the line, its members in casual mode. Great lengths of cloth are employed as camouflage against French and British aerial observation.

GWG14_236. A German officer addresses marines before their return to the front. The trigger area of each man's rifle has been covered, a precaution against the sight and breech becoming blocked with sand.

GWG14_231. German officers stand on the ornate steps of a 'Mairie et Justice de Paix' – that is the town hall and the equivalent of a magistrates' court.

GWG14_240. A German dug out, supported by wickerwork, lined internally with log beams and with timber supports; layered bundles of branches waterproof the roof.

GWG14_244. German gunners in front of a well built wooden shelter (Villa Fliegerlod). From the main entrance there is a chest-high trench in which stand an officer and NCO.

GWG14_243. Two German officers, comfortably ensconced, consider the news from the home front.

GWG14_242. Gunners visit the latrine: squatting safely behind the line, unconcernedly engaged in conversation, some reading regional German newspapers, which would also make up for the lack of toilet paper.

GWG14_250. Wicker shell baskets and ammunition boxes lie abandoned by the roadside in France.

GWG14_241. A German artillery section in a trench lined with wicker in the Verdun sector; it was some time before this was replaced by corrugated iron sheets. The NCO, front row standing, third from right, wears his ribbon of the Iron Cross, second class.

GWG14_246. A German officer and other ranks, all recipients of the Iron Cross, monitor enemy positions from behind the line, using various types of range finding equipment.

GWG14_247. German soldiers 'at rest' on a river bank in northern France.

GWG14_248. Lock gates damaged by German artillery; the lock keeper's lodge has clearly received a direct hit.

GWG14_253. Formerly a verdant hillside forest, now a barren wasteland of shattered tree stumps and pockmarked terrain.

GWG14_251. An unknown dead soldier in the centre of the photograph, probably a victim of shelling, lies amid the devastated remains of an entrenchment dug in what was once a wood.

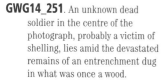

GWG14_254. A snow-lined, duck-boarded German trench, France.

GWG14_255. A German trench in northern France; the heap of iron spikes at the bottom of the trench are stakes that will be used to support barbed wire entanglements.

GWG14_249. German shelling has laid waste this village in north eastern France.

GWG14_260. A French Dumezil 58mm trench mortar round (No.2 pattern).

GWG14_259. Stockpiled: a dump of French Dumezil 58mm trench mortar rounds, abandoned by retreating French troops.

GWG14_258. German infantry digging inside a cellar, filling sandbags.

GWG14_252. A French Dumezil 58mm trench mortar bomb (No.2 pattern) lying at the bottom of a trench abandoned by retiring French forces.

GWG14_257. Infantrymen of the 83rd (3rd Kurhessian) Infantry Regiment 'von Wittich' survey No Man's Land. The soldier with the rifle is wearing a Brandenburg cuff – characterised by three buttons running vertically up the sleeve.

GWG14_256. A German officer walks along a trench in northern France, at some time in 1916 or later.

GWG14_261. A German 210mm Mörser 16 heavy howitzer, partially screened by vegetation, fires a round.

GWG14_265. German 'mounted' infantry transport supplies, using donkeys to pull their carts.

GWG14_262. A destroyed battery of Belgian field guns, 120mm L de Bange Mle. All the breech screws and locks have been removed, frustrating any attempt to fire the weapons on their former owners.

GWG14_264. A view from the opposite side: two German non-commissioned officers (on the far left a Feldwebel, on the right an Unteroffizier) stand in the sprawling encampment of Totermann Mühle *lager*.

GWG14_263. Totermann Mühle, the German-built lakeside depot established near Binarville, along the river L'Homme Mort.

GWG14_269. The German occupation: an Unteroffizier in the German infantry poses, resting on his walking stick, in a village in northern France.

GWG14_270. German troops in occupation: on the right is a temporary *Bayerische Kantine* (Bavarian canteen), installed in what was the post office.

GWG14_268. A panoramic view of a town in northern France.

GWG14_266. Artillery has destroyed a bridge in northern France. However, the railway bridge is still in operation, permitting the transportation of both goods and men.

GWG14_267. An undamaged hamlet in north eastern France occupied by German forces.

GWG14_273. A wartime photograph captures the tranquil, rural, almost bucolic, atmosphere of an occupied French village.

GWG14_274. German troops salute and wave at Kaiser Wilhelm II, who is in the back of the motorcar.

GWG14_275. Wrecked by shells – the interior of a church in northern France.

GWG14_271. French prisoners, under guard, maintain the roads in northern France. Behind them is a large French house, built in 1747, now commandeered for the use of the Second Reich.

GWG14_272. German troops – one leaning heavily on a walking stick – mingle freely with the inhabitants of an undamaged village in northern France.

GWG14_276. The exterior of a bomb-damaged church – closed for renovations – in northern France.Churches were common targets for the artillery of both sides – easily identifiable and often providing excellent places for observers in their towers: consequently they were often more badly damaged than the village or town in which they stood.

GWG14_279. The destructive power of artillery fire is shown in this photograph of a village in France after a German bombardment.

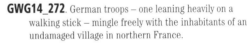

GWG14_278. A small French school and garden in north west France, slightly damaged by German shells.

GWG14_285. A German infantry machine gunner scans the horizon with his Maxim MG 08 (Maschinengewehr 08), using the stump of a tree as a makeshift mounting.

GWG14_277. A German cemetery in northern France; the inscription above the gate reads 'J. R. 120 Friedhof' (the Cemetery of the 120th Infantry Regiment).

GWG14_284. Crew members and mechanics stand beside a 1911 Daimler 4x4, with 7.7cm BAK – *Plattform-wagen* – a pre-war adaptation of the mobile flak wagon.

GWG14_281. Two German NCOs – on the right, an
Unteroffizier gunner – sit astride the barrel of an
artillery piece.

GWG14_282. Two gunners of the German army,
both awarded the Iron Cross, enjoying some time
relaxing behind the line.

GWG14_283. Beachhead: barbed wire entanglements
run the length of an unknown beach in northern
France.

GWG14_280. Further scenes of destruction along a quiet
country lane: shattered trees and damaged houses.

GWG14_288. A group of German infantrymen pose for a rather 'stiff' group photograph, despite the presence of beer steins.

GWG14_287. A very relaxed German soldier, dressed for the worst that the weather can throw at him, stands amidst the rubble and debris of a French village.

GWG14_286. A studio portrait of a decorated – Iron Cross second class – non-commissioned officer of the German artillery.

Chapter Three:
Vormarsch nach Osten und Ruckmarsch
(Advance in the East and Withdrawal)

'The Serbs must be disposed of, and that right soon!'

On 23 July 1914, following the assassination of Archduke Ferdinand and his wife almost a month earlier, the Austro-Hungarian government presented an ultimatum to the Serbian government. It demanded, amongst other things: the suppression of all inflammatory publications and anti Austro-Hungarian propaganda; the dissolution of Serbian nationalist societies; a judicial inquiry into the assassination plot of 28 June; and the immediate arrests of Major Voja Tankosić and Milan Ciganović. The murder of the Archduke had inflamed political and military feelings in Vienna – and the guarantee of German support seemed to make war all but inevitable; Conrad von Hötzendorf, the Austrian Chief of the General Staff, viewed the assassination as a heaven sent opportunity to deal with Serbia, the supporter of Slav unrest in Austria's sprawling Balkan and eastern empire.

On 25 July the Serbs responded by accepting all but one of the conditions of the ultimatum – that is, Item Six, a judicial inquiry on the events of 28 June in Serbia undertaken by Austrian judicial officials. On 28 July Austria-Hungary, dissatisfied with the Serb response, declared war and proceeded to shell Belgrade the following morning. The Tsar, who considered himself – and thus by extension considered Russia – the safeguard of the Slav peoples, on 30 July reluctantly approved the full scale mobilisation of his forces for action against Germany and Austro-Hungary as a consequence of the shelling. In reply, Germany declared war on Russia on 1 August.

The whole basis of the strategy of the Central Powers had been on the premise that Russia would be slow to mobilise and even slower to have an effective field army in place; the gap would allow for France and any of her allies to be knocked out of the war before Russia, in turn, was dealt with. Small Serbia would, it was thought, be rapidly removed from the war.

The Eastern Front, even by as early as the end of 1914, developed into a very different military experience from the situation on the Western Front. On the latter the war seemed to have settled into a stalemate by Christmas, symbolised by a line of trenches from the North Sea to Switzerland. In the East the line could – and often did – oscillate considerable distances as the fortunes of war dictated. The length of the front line was far greater, the country vaster and much more open and less developed, field fortifications tended to be more primitive than the Western counterparts – a war of movement was always possible throughout the conflict.

The German army was the best prepared of the protagonists; the main issue facing the Austro-

Hungarian army – *Kaiserlich und Königlich* (k.und k.) [Imperial and Royal] – was its sheer ethnic diversity, as a significant proportion of its composite peoples were actively seeking their individual national independence. Russia's army had the men but, despite breathtakingly speedy industrialisation and development of railway infrastructure in the years before the war, was ill equipped and supplied and with a totally inadequate munitions industry. Neither Austria nor Russia was prepared for a major conflict in the summer of 1914.

Thus it was a major surprise to the Germans when the Russians launched an invasion of East Prussia – the part that might be described as German Poland – on 12 August with two armies; with a remarkably speedy advance they then invaded East Prussia proper on 17 August. Meanwhile, four other Russian armies prepared to invade the Austrian territory of Galicia. On 18 August the Russian First Army came upon a corps of the German Eighth Army (von Prittwitz), which with only nine divisions was tasked with defence of the east, and forced its withdrawal to Gumbinnen. Prittwitz was to be the first senior commander of either side to be dismissed, replaced by Hindenburg and Ludendorf on 22 August, though in fact it was his plan (or, rather, that of his chief of staff, Max Hoffman) that was adopted that resulted in the decisive victory, fought over several days, that is known to history, somewhat misleadingly, as the Battle of Tannenberg. But the damage to the German effort on the Western Front had already been done, as two invaluable corps were entrained on 26 August for transfer to the east – where they arrived too late to effect anything.

The Austrians also had considerable early successes against the Russians and all looked well for the Central Powers in the east – the Russian willingness to advance before her armies were fully prepared looked as though it might prove to be a fatal mistake. However, Conrad had over-extended his armies and been too ambitious and the Russian Fifth Army soon had the Austrians on the back foot in Galicia and facing the real danger of encirclement. By the end of August the Germans had restored their situation; but the Austrians had been forced back two hundred miles and suffered 350,000 casualties.

Austria's plans for Serbia had been disrupted by Russia's unexpected – and successful – belligerence, so that forces earmarked to deal with her troublesome Balkan neighbour had to be deployed elsewhere. Austria invaded Serbia on 12 August and had some initial success. But the Serbs were determined to save their homeland, knew the terrain well and fought with fanatical bravery. By the end of the year the 500,000 or so troops that Austria had deployed had been, more or less, ejected from Serbia and about a half of them had become casualties.

Not that the Germans had all that much to crow over, as Hindenburg fought a disastrous battle around Warsaw and Russian troops returned to East Prussia. Indeed, in 1914 Russia's army, despite everything, had performed very well. The outcome of the fighting in the east was profound, as Falkenhayn, the new (since September) German Chief of the General Staff, made the fateful decision to concentrate Germany's efforts for 1915 on the Eastern Front.

GWG14_290. A German machine gun team from the safety of a trench watches the movements of Russian infantrymen.

GWG14_289. In retreat, Russian troops put to flame a Polish town rather than allow stockpiles of grain and wheat to fall into enemy hands.

GWG14_291. A pause in the fighting: German soldiers stationed in Poland enjoy a moment of relaxation in the autumn sun.

GWG14_293. A German machine gun section at the Battle of Tannenburg looks to the front, screened by the defence of a squat stone wall and rampant mass of vegetation. With the coming winter and ice on the ground it was impracticable to dig set entrenchments.

GWG14_297. Three newcomers to *der Ostfront* pose for the photographer in their shallow trench, which could only have provided the most rudimentary of protection, a clear sign of the distance between the two combatants.

GWG14_294. Two machine guns, both equipped with a protective armoured shield, guard a section of the line. Note the dense (for this early in the war) barbed wire defences. Note that the four men closest to the camera all carry a leather belt with metal 'cuffs' at the end over their left shoulders. This was used to facilitate the carrying of the Maxim MG08. The belt served to develop the myth in the later stages of the war that German machine gunners chained themselves to their weapons.

GWG14_292. A makeshift band of musicians and instruments led by the inevitable accordion entertain the inhabitants of a village in Russian Poland.

GWG14_296. German heavy artillery positioned on the outlying fringe of Lodz bombards the city.

GWG14_295. German cavalry on the move.

GWG14_298. A German encampment near the Russian frontier.

GWG14_300. The officers' quarters: Austrian officers enjoy a period of respite whilst serving on the Eastern Front.

GWG14_299. Kaiser Wilhelm II (far left) addresses General von Mackensen (centre) in East Prussia. The officer standing to attention to the far left is a member of the Death's Head Hussars (*Totenkopf-Husaren*).

GWG14_301. With their task completed, Austrian engineers sit for the camera astride a suspension bridge constructed across an unknown river on the Eastern Front.

GWG14_302. German soldiers stationed in Tannenburg requisition all available provisions, foodstuffs and household items in the area.

GWG14_304. Two stretcher-cases receive medical attention before being conveyed to hospital.

GWG14_303. A staged photograph: German infantry with bayonets fixed swarm en masse from support line trenches into No Man's Land.

GWG14_310. Shells (known as Black Marias) in wicker transport and protective cases, lie ready for transport to batteries. Each shell weighed 760 pounds.

GWG14_308. Employed as scouts in Russian Poland, German soldiers carrying news of the battle pay visits to friends and family close to the Russian-German border.

GWG14_305. German infantry, alert, watch the movements of enemy troops from the safety of hillside woodland.

GWG14_307. Three soldiers sit waiting for a haircut. Note the improvised equipment rack (background left), a low-hanging branch of a convenient pine tree.

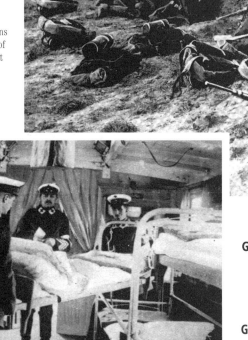

GWG14_306. German troops dig in to provide some basic shelter. It was some time before earthworks on the Eastern Front developed into more formidable defensive positions – and even then the nature of the fighting there meant that these never reached the complexity of those on the Western Front.

GWG14_311. Two supervised medics add a stretcher bunk to the complement on the carriage of a hospital train.

GWG14_309. Germany infantry of the 12th (2nd Brandenburg) Grenadiers 'Prince Charles of Prussia', rest in the recently cut hay of a farmer's field.

GWG14_315. Russian PoWs in transit by train take a short break under close German supervision. The side of the carriage is covered in crude graffiti, written and drawn.

GWG14_312. A wolf in sheep's clothing: a German sentry in a winter sheep skin coat stands guard over ammunition wagons.

GWG14_314. A destroyed Russian aircraft is transported to a German airfield; the caption informs us that the engine would be transferred for use in a German aircraft, which would seem a rather perilous thing to do.

GWG14_316. Russian soldiers being marched through the streets to their PoW camp.

GWG14_313. A German forage wagon stuck on a muddy Polish road.

GWG14_317. Scene in the market pace of Philippovo, East Prussia: the *Landsturm* officer (pictured centre middle) interrogates a civilian charged with petty theft.

GWG14_318. An outpost line of the Tsar's Polish troops, protected by nothing more than scrapes in the ground, await the arrival of troops from the Central Powers.

GWG14_319. An Austrian and German officer, under the watchful eye of Austrian troops, inspects a mobile Russia Oulemet Maksima Obrazets Model 1910 (PM Model 1910) heavy machine gun, mounted temporarily aboard a cart. The PM Model 1910 was a licensed 7.62mm Russian Empire copy of the famous Maxim design.

GWG14_322. A German officer and his men in pursuit of a Russian spy enter a Polish farmhouse in which they believe he has taken refuge.

GWG14_321. Outpost duty: Austrian troops enjoy a period of rest, several of them reading illustrated magazines. Both sides produced these popular journals in abundance, pictorially depicting what was happening in the war, often with a great degree of literary licence.

GWG14_320. Battle weary German soldiers snatch an uncomfortable rest in an inn in East Prussia.

GWG14_323. General von Gropp and his chief of staff inspect the battlefield. The soldiers in the foreground are part of an MG 08 crew.

GWG14_327. Sleigh ambulance: Germans, wounded while fighting on the Russian frontier, are carted to the rear on an improvised hospital sleigh.

GWG14_326. A German officer surveys the enemy line with his binoculars from the safety of a well constructed trench, with extensive wooden supports.

GWG14_324. A citizen of East Prussia offers refreshment – possibly in exchange for money – to a band of German cavalry, stationed briefly in this small hamlet.

GWG14_325. Commandeering bread for the Kaiser's men: a detachment of the German Commissariat Korps make a bread levy from a bakery in East Prussia.

GWG14_328. Austrian reinforcements (reservists) move over snow covered ground to join the forward positions of their army in Serbia.

GWG14_330. Austrian troops on the alert from a very crowded looking earthwork in the Carpathian Mountains.

GWG14_329. Austrian mountain troops, equipped with skis, make use of a precarious bridge to cross a river in the Carpathian Mountains.

GWG14_332. An Austrian artillery battery in the field; during times of war a field battery consisted of six guns, in peacetime only four.

GWG14_334. Siege howitzer: A contemporary illustration of an Austrian Škoda 305 mm Model 1911 howitzer being readied to fire. A crew of 15 to 17 men was required to fire the artillery piece.

GWG14_335. Gunners push a carriage holding a 305mm (12inch) shell to its gun. The shell for this gun was manufactured in light (633lb) and heavy (847lb) types, the former fitted with an impact fuse.

GWG14_333. Austrian engineers putting the finishing touches to a trestle bridge across a river in the foothills of the Carpathian Mountains. Notice the giant mallet held by a soldier on the right of the group in the foreground.

GWG14_331. Modified motor lorries – note the presence of railroad car wheels in lieu of the standard transport wheel – traverse a section of the ascending Carpathian Mountain railroad.

GWG14_336. Austrian troops encamped in the Carpathian Mountains await orders.

GWG14_337. Munitions transportation: ammunition is conveyed to the front by mule.

GWG14_338. The Archduke Charles of Austria (to become Emperor Charles I on the death of Emperor Franz Jozef in 1916) inspects some of his troops in Poland.

WG14_340. Russian infantry escort Austrian PoWs to the rear. The absence of snow on the ground would suggest that this photograph was taken during the first months of the campaign in Galicia.

GWG14_339. Austrian dead killed at the Battle of Kielce are gathered before their burial.

GWG14_ 344. The Austrian Garrison of Przemysl, besieged by enemy forces. A group of Austrian officers consult a map.

GWG14_341. Austrian (heavy) artillery in action beside a lake in Galicia.

GWG14_342. Austrian motorcyclists, deployed as despatch riders, parade by their bikes, a collection of varying models.

GWG14_343. A street scene in Przemysl – two officers are followed by a wounded soldier and his two helpers.

GWG14_345. Austrian trenches in Galicia. A suspiciously 'clean' scene of a part of the line, with front line and communications trenches and buildings untouched, it would appear, by the war.

GWG14_346. A battery of Austrian heavy howitzers.

GWG14_347. Hungarian *Landwehr* (*Honvéd*) march towards their transport for the front, watched by a large number of civilians.

GWG14_348. Reservists and volunteers, making their way to army depots, answer the call to the colours in Vienna.

GWG14_351. Austrian artillery 'engage the enemy', employing a number of 8 cm Feldkanone M 05 (8 cm FK M. 5) field guns. The white conical tents in the background suggest that this is merely a training exercise.

GWG14_349. Austrian engineers – almost certainly specialist bridging troops – complete a pontoon bridge across the Danube.

GWG14_350. Austrian field artillery advancing in formation on an exercise.

GWG14_352. Austrian mounted battery.

GWG14_353. The interior of a
hospital train compartment,
along with some of its
attendants.

GWG14_354. A Hungarian infantry battalion poses for the camera;
given the generally relaxed air, this was almost certainly taken
during field training.

GWG14_356. Various types of soldier in the *KuK* (Imperial and Royal) army from the different parts of the Austro-Hungarian Empire, including gunners, infantry, cavalry and marines.

GWG14_355. An Austrian battalion, equipped in review order, on the march.

GWG14_357. The Archduke Franz Ferdinand, whose assassination provided the spark for the war, addressing Austrian infantry who had been engaged in field exercises.

GWG14_358. Officers swearing allegiance in the forecourt of the military academy in Vienna.

GWG14_359. Austrian Škoda 305 mm Model 1911 howitzer in action in the Carpathians: such guns could be used only where a concrete setting was possible.

GWG14_362. Polish infantry at rest in the Carpathians, given their lack of equipment readily to hand, presumably well behind the lines.

GWG14_361. Caltrops and barbed wire: staked pits – varying in depth and interval – and wire entanglements present a formidable obstacle to any would-be aggressor.

GWG14_360. Emperor Franz Josef I, who ruled Austria and her empire from 1848 to 1916.

GWG14_364. Polish cavalry in the Kaiser's service; the historic kingdom of Poland did not exist as a country, because it was split between Germany, Austria and Russia.

GWG14_363. Archduke Charles, heir to the Austro-Hungarian thrones, visiting the Austrian Headquarters at Przemyl, a city which suffered a massive siege operation by the Russians in late 1914 and 1915.

GWG14_366. Austrian sentry guards a railway line somewhere on the Galician frontier.

GWG14_365. Archduke Charles is assisted by the commanding general at Przemyl, whilst an aide seems to be offering advice.

GWG14_367. Austrian troops (mountain troops, to judge by the skis most of them carry) entraining for the front at a stop outside the Arsenal in Vienna.

GWG14_368. Austrian engineers operate a field telegraph in Poland.

GWG14_371. A German officer and an Austrian infantryman stand together outside a farmhouse in East Galicia.

GWG14_370. Austrian command post installed in a farmhouse in East Galicia.

GWG14_372. 4 February 1914: a German officer, a recipient of the Iron Cross, second class, sits meditatively amid the comfort of a recently vacated peasant homestead, smoking a cigar.

GWG14_373. German and Austrian commissioned and non-commissioned officers relax in the comfort of a recently vacated home in East Galicia.

GWG14_369. General Rudolf Stögger-Steiner and his staff observe operations in Galicia.

GWG14_374. German and Austrian infantry officers enjoy a drink in their mess. Note that the officer second from right has the Iron Cross.

GWG14_376. Two infantrymen, one Austrian and one German, play with two foals.

GWG14_377. An Austrian soldier with a horse and foal in East Galicia.

GWG14_375. Two young volunteers plough a field in Russian Poland, employing a pair of captured farm animals.

GWG14_378. In the midst of war … A hen and her chicks go about their usual search for food.

GWG14_379. A group of schoolchildren, probably playing at soldiers, are supervised by a *leutnant* – note the officer's collar tabs – of the German infantry. The ribbon in his buttonhole indicates that he olds the Iron Cross Second Class.

GWG14_381. A woman in East Galicia tends her cow, watering the beast at the local stream.

GWG14_382. A 150mm heavy howitzer in its firing position and protected by a tarpaulin against the icy weather.

GWG14_380. Boys – army cadets – stand to attention beside two soldiers of the German Army.

GWG14_383. Party games: Austrian infantry in sacks attempt to grab bread attached to strings tied to a pole.

GWG14_384. Austrian engineers construct a swimming bath, using a nearby river to fill it. Keeping men clean and lice free was a permanent battle for all the combatants.

GWG14_385. Before entering the communal baths via a sluice gate the soldiers are offered bars of soap.

GWG14_386. Besides washing themselves, wooden rails have been erected, which enabled the men to wash and dry their clothes.

GWG14_387. Three German soldiers, in Russian Poland, enjoy the view.

GWG14_388. Austrian troops stand in line for a meal, somewhere in Russian Poland.

GWG14_389. Austrian artillery bombards Russian positions in Galicia during a night time shoot.

GWG14_391. A church in Galicia in flames after being struck by a Russian shell, the flames standing out starkly against the night.

GWG14_390. Fire rages uncontrollably, destroying a house in Galicia.

GWG14_393. A German officer wearing a fur lined greatcoat stands amid the ruin of a farmer's house in Russian Poland.

GWG14_392. A Russian shell burst, seemingly well off target.

GWG14_394. Austrian engineers construct a stone platform on the Eastern Front.

GWG14_395. Three German soldiers (the one standing on the right is both a recipient of the Iron Cross, second class and an Unteroffizier) installed in a log cabin, Galicia, pose for the camera; a cluster of infantry rifles leans against the wall of the entrance porch.

GWG14_396. A German *leutnant* (equivalent to a second lieutenant) of Infanterie Regiment Nr 15 (2nd Westphalian) scans No Man's Land through trench binoculars, SF14 G Scherenfernrohr 14, understandably known to the soldiers as 'rabbit ears'.

GWG14_398. A senior Austrian officer and his aides prepare to set off in their staff car.

GWG14_399. Even generals have to parade. These Austrian and German generals greet a visiting dignitary; note that at least three of them have the Iron Cross First Class.

GWG14_397. A German officer, complete with walking stick, leans nonchalantly against the railings of a bridge that has also been designed to carry a light railway.

GWG14_400. German infantry march past a group of senior Austrian and German generals. Note that the photograph must date from 1917, as the steel helmet was not issued on the Eastern Front until well into that year.

GWG14_401. A well developed defensive position on a quiet part of the Eastern Front.

GWG14_404. A well developed defence work, constructed by Austrian engineers, crosses wetland.

GWG14_403. Men of the *Honvéd*, Hungarian *Landwehr* – notice the 'H' stencilled to the forage cap of the man second from the right – and a dog sit for the camera in a wicker-lined trench in East Galicia.

GWG14_402. Austrian mountain infantry – as shown by the edelweiss patch sewn to the collar of the *Zugsführer* (platoon sergeant) seated behind the Schwarzlose MG M.07/12 – pose for the camera in a wicker-lined trench along a quiet sector of the Eastern front.

GWG14_405. A German soldier studies an expanse of woodland in front of this well-fortified entrenchment – fire step, parapet and walls have all been 'revetted' with wood branches, woven and bound together to support the trench sides, a practice common in many German trenches.

GWG14_406. German infantry – an MG 08 Maxim nestled behind the soldier far left – pose for the camera embedded in a trench in East Prussia.

GWG14_407. Austrian infantry sport a varied array of captured headgear – including two fur lined Cossack hats and two of the French 'Adrian' helmets, which gradually came into service in late 1915 and was also used by the Russian army.

GWG14_408. A group of recently called up men in their barracks room, holding a variety of items, from a shovel, a brush and bayonet to a couple of lucky ones with a beer.

GWG14_411. Back to the past and the Age of Reason: a German officer and his bride pose in eighteenth century costume; interesting to note that the man is wearing high heels, then the height of masculine fashion.

GWG14_409. A mixed group of infantry and cavalry on the move in Russian Poland.

GWG14_410. A supply column and its drivers pause for a rest; the horses have been removed from their traces, presumably to be watered and fed.

GWG14_412. Russian victims of battle lie in a wooded area.

GWG14_413. *Gefechte vor der Linie Stellung*: German infantry in rudimentary cover in the midst of undamaged countryside: a scene from the late autumn in Russian Poland. The great length of the Eastern Front meant that complex trench systems were generally slower in being developed than in the West, except where the fighting was most severe.

GWG14_414. Russian dead on the battlefield.

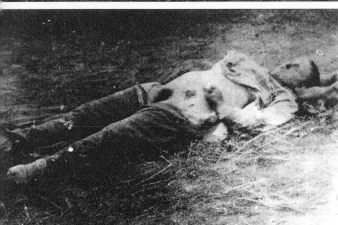

GWG14_415. The partially stripped corpse of a Russian soldier.

GWG14_416. A german soldier engages in foolery with an oversized 'pipe'.

GWG14_417. Barracks under construction for the German army in Galicia.

GWG14_418. Two German soldiers view the damage wrought by Russian shelling on a five storey building.

GWG14_419. Rifle inspection – a daily ritual for all infantry but these Germans seem happier than most about the chore.

GWG14_420. German engineers (an officer and an NCO) paddle near a newly constructed bridge built by the Germans.

GWG14_421. A family outing on the water; the son (an officer) is in the bow whilst his father is doing the work.

GWG14_422. A group of German soldiers (two with the Iron Cross), forming a semi circle around the carcass of a pig, looking forward to some pork.

GWG14_423. A group photograph of German troops making the most of their lakeside location for a bathe.

GWG14_424. Possibly with visions of Hollywood, a member of Infanterie-Regiment Nr 106 (7th Royal Saxon 'King George'), smiles at the camera.

GWG14_425. Champagne: a miscellaneous crowd of officers and infantrymen queue patiently at a Verkauf nur an Pioniere (Pioneers only shop).

Chapter Four:
Kriegschauplatz Asien und Afrika
(The Pacific and African Theatres)

'In all the German colonies, though but a few decades old, a life full of promise was discernible. We were beginning to understand the national value of our Colonial possessions.'

In 1880 sub Saharan Africa was one of the last regions of the world to be untouched by 'informal' imperialism – that is a creeping colonisation based on coastal trading stations. At this date only some ten percent of African soil was under European control (and much of that was in the west and south); by 1900 that figure was to rise to ninety percent. The last decades of the nineteenth century showed a revived colonial thirst and not only amongst the traditional colonising European powers, as Germany, Italy, Japan and the United States joined the club. The reasons for this centred on two principal issues: colonies were equated with national prestige and an international reach; and the need for secure coaling stations for navies that had become steam powered; whilst economic possibilities were also a consideration, with some parts of the continent being of more significance in this respect than others.

The Conference of Berlin of 1884 and 1885 and subsequent bilateral agreements settled, to a large degree, a number of territorial colonial squabbles, particularly in Africa, which had degenerated into 'the Scramble for Africa'; and almost entirely to the satisfaction of the British.

In Africa Germany, in 1914, controlled: Togoland (now Togo and in part of Ghana); Cameroon; German East Africa (Tangyanika – not modern Tanzania, which includes the then British protectorate of Zanzibar, modern Burundi and Rwanda); and South West Africa (Namibia). In Oceania – or the Pacific: New Guinea (German Papua New Guinea); Samoa; the concessionary post of Tsingtao (Quindao, China); Neu Pommern – the largest island in the Bismarck Archipelago; the Caroline, Marshall and Solomon Islands; Mariana; Nauru and Bougainville. Unlike France and Britain, Germany did relatively little to mould its new colonial subjects, regarding the colonies as of strategic importance only as regards their location and otherwise as possessions for adventurous German settlers. These colonies, as was the experience of most of the other colonial powers as regards these new additions, were generally a financial burden and of little economic significance.

The Germans were almost certainly under no illusion as to the viability of these outposts in a war involving Britain, France and Japan as enemies. However, British attempts to take German East Africa were foiled by a dogged resistance that outlasted German efforts everywhere else in the world; the surrender of her forces there came almost a fortnight after the Armistice was signed in France. The other dependencies fell rapidly. The new Union of South Africa over-ran German South West Africa by the summer of 1915. Japanese forces, aided by a small contribution of British, Indian and Australian troops and naval assets, eventually overcame a dogged defence of Tsingtao by German and Austrian soldiers and sailors that endured for almost two months

GWG14_426. Yaoundé club, used by the Germans as an ammunition factory.

GWG14_427. The Banyo Band march ahead of a military column in South-West Africa.

GWG14_428. German infantry officers inspect a contingent of colonial troops in the background is the German fort of Mora.

GWG14_429. A pre-war photograph captures the arrival of the German governor at Banyo.

GWG14_430. Mounted German officers inspect colonial troops stationed at the Banyo station.

GWG14_432. A group of locally recruited native troops (askaris), with their German officer in the middle.

GWG14_433. A line of fully equipped German askaris, out on exercise.

GWG14_434. German native cavalry in their full dress uniform.

GWG14_436. The German fort of Kusseri was captured by French troops in the early hours of 25 September 1914.

GWG14_435. The Yaboma bridge. The central structure (pictured midpoint) is part way through repair, the bridge having originally been destroyed as a preventative measure against attack.

GWG14_437. A tree-lined avenue in the European quarter of Duala.

GWG14_438. Fort Lolodorf, eighty miles southwest of Yaoundé, Cameroons.

GWG14_440. Askaris at musketry practice on the range.

GWG14_441. Askaris being drilled on the square.

GWG14_439. A chief of the German Cameroons poses for the camera in his tribal finery and head-dress.

GWG14_446. General Louis Botha, Prime Minister of the Union of South Africa, presents the terms of surrender to local German commanders in German South West Africa.

GWG14_443. Musketry drill: African infantry practice firing the German-built M 98 (*Gewehr* 98).

GWG14_442. African troops rehearse the characteristic 'goose-step' past a Gefreiter (lance-corporal).

GWG14_444. Colonial troops queue for their turn on the high beam.

GWG14_445. German askaris rehearse column of route on the drill square.

GWG14_448. A German soldier makes use of an unusual ride, a zebra, in Dar es Salaam, German East Africa.

GWG14_447. A column of the German Colonial Camel Korps of German South West Africa.

GWG14_450. A German signals section, based on the fortress walls of a garrison at Tsingtao (China) use a heliograph to signal to other troops out on patrol.

GWG14_449. A contemporary street scene taken in Lome, the port of Togoland and now the capital of Togo

GWG14_452. Japanese infantry cross a river as troops close in on the German garrison at Tsingtao.

GWG14_451. Indian Army troops transport ammunition for the Japanese forces besieging the Germans in Tsingtao.

GWG14_453. Japanese soldiers enjoy a meal of rice at a base established on the outskirts of Tsingtao.

GWG14_454. The wireless station established at Tsingtao after heavy shelling by the enemy.

GWG14_455. Oil tanks destroyed as a result of allied shelling, Tsingtao.

GWG14_456. The German Imperial Eagle carved on stone on the heights overlooking Tsingtao.

GWG14_457. A contemporary photograph captures an everyday street scene under German rule in Tsingtao.

GWG14_458. The Central Hotel and skating rink pictured from the pier at the Kiao-chau German naval base.

GWG14_459. Chinese residents, natives of Tsingtao, sift beans.

GWG14_460. Native boot makers display their wares at market, Tsingtao.

GWG14_461. The market place of Papeete, Tahiti, subsequent to German naval shelling – an attack carried out by the *Scharnhorst* and *Gneisenau*, German cruisers, on 22 September.

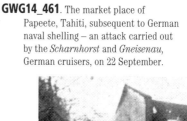

GWG14_462. A store at Papeete, Tahiti, destroyed in the bombardment by the *Scharnhorst* and *Gneisenau*. The two cruisers fired some 150 shells in their raid.

GWG14_463. The Governor's bungalow Herbertshöhe, Bismarck Archipelago.

GWG14_465. A gaping hole in a Port Trust warehouse (guarded by a British corporal), the result of shelling by the German light cruiser *Emden*.

GWG14_464. Oil tanks, the property of the Burmah Oil Company burn heavily at Madras, the result of naval shelling by the German light cruiser *Emden*.

GWG14_466. A column of marines of the German III *Seebattalion* marching through the streets of Tsingtao.

GWG14_469. A marine outpost position, including a machine gun and crew. The officer, to the left of the gun, is equipped with the long barrelled artillery Lug P08 (Parabellum). So also is a marine, front row and to his left, who is also carrying an army issue bugle.

GWG14_468. A view from behind the position in Photograph 468 and which shows the complete gun team.

GWG14_467. Marines equipped with a MG 08 machine gun man an entrenched post in outer defences of Tsingtao.

GWG14_470. The port of Tsingato, China, pictured prior to the Japanese blockade on 24 August 1914.

GWG14_471. Apia, the capital of German Samoa.

Chapter Five:
Türkei (Turkey)

The Anatolian Turk is 'courageous…a first-class fighting soldier'. He is limited,
however, 'by his poor education and consequent inability to handle complex
weapons and equipment'.

The Ottoman Empire had been on an erratic path of decline since its western territorial expansion had reached its apogee at the Siege of Vienna in 1688. The nineteenth century was dominated by various rebellions and wars of independence in its European possessions – at first in Greece and subsequently in the Balkans. Many of the seeds and, indeed, the flame for the First World War were to be found in the complex political and military rivalries between emerging regional powers and whose antics much preoccupied the Great Powers in the years preceding the outbreak of the First World War.

At home there was revolution in the air, with the so-called Young Turk movement launching a coup against the traditional government of the Sultan; followed by a split in the movement and a power struggle, ending in early 1913. It was vigorous and determined to bring Turkey into the realities of the twentieth century; and its leaders, notably Enver Pasha, were ambitious for Turkey's place in the world. Most threatened by Russia (although also with an unhealthy rivalry with Greece), it suited Germany's strategic interests to build on this fear; which was achieved by diplomatic overtures and the construction of the Berlin-Baghdad railway (though not completed until 1940), along with a sizeable military staff attached to the Turkish army.

The modernisation and rebuilding of the Ottoman army was a work in progress in 1914; it had suffered some bruising recent encounters, not least in the recent Second Balkan War. However, with German military aid – including the provision of the Chief of the General Staff – it was making substantial progress and was a far more formidable potential foe than it had been a couple of years earlier. From Germany's point of view an alliance with Turkey, along with an existing one with Bulgaria, would provide strategically valuable internal lines of communication for the Central Powers; whilst it would also threaten British colonial and economic interests – i.e. the Suez Canal zone and even the land route to India.

Despite the affinity with Germany and even a treaty of (conditional) alliance, signed as recently as 2 August, it was far from clear which direction Turkey would take when war broke out in early August in Europe. The risks were considerable. The Turks (and particularly as regards the security of the capital, Constantinople/Istanbul) felt vulnerable to the might of the Royal Navy; of the very lengthy border with Russia to the north; whilst some of the Central

Powers' allies had been her enemies just a couple of years earlier – there was much to play for in the struggle to secure Turkish support.

The British decision not to deliver two capital warships at the outbreak of war was seized upon by the Germans, who gifted the Ottomans with two on 11 August; a massive propaganda coup. Enver Pasha, the Defence Minister, won the power struggle within the Turkish government and with his support the balance fell on Germany's side. War was declared against Russia, not by note but by the bombardment and sinking of Russian vessels on 28 and 29 October, hitting the major naval ports of Sebastapol and Odessa.

GWG14_472. The debris of a Turkish defeat after the German inspired attack on the Suez Canal Zone (including crossing the canal in pontoons) resulted in disastrous failure.

GWG14_473. Turkish citizens march proudly into Constantinople to join the colours.

GWG14_474. Bedouin infantry march past in review order before representatives of the Ottoman government.

GWG14_475. Turkish cavalry depart for the front.

GWG14_477. A crowd gathers to witness the reading of the proclamation of the Holy War.

GWG14_476. Reservists from Palestine (on the far left) pass regulars of the Turkish army in the shadow of the Sultan Ahmed Mosque.

GWG14_478. Following the formal entry into the war of the Ottoman Empire on the side of the Central Powers, in Istanbul Sheikh-ul-Islam proclaims a Holy War.

GWG14_480. Anatolian men waiting to be processed through the recruiting system.

GWG14_479. The Heir Assumptive to the Ottoman throne outside a tent.

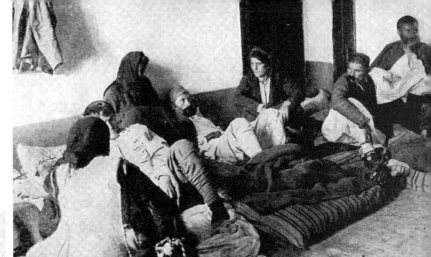

GWG14_481. Turkish wounded being cared for in fairly rudimentary conditions.

GWG14_482. Members of an Ottoman Arab division moving towards the front.

GWG14_484. Turkish artillery on manoeuvres.

GWG14_483. Turkish emissaries in Berlin.

GWG14_486. Turkish soldiers being ferried across the Euphrates in a rubber dinghy; note that it is a woman who is doing all the work!

GWG14_485. An instructor demonstrates to his pupils how to grip and hold the German manufactured service rifle M 98. Perhaps one instruction should have been that it is not best practice to stand in front of the barrel of a weapon.

GWG14_488. Military supplies are transported to the front by camel across the desert.

GWG14_490. Two gunners of the Turkish artillery sit abreast on a German-made 7.7 cm Feldkanone 96 neuer Art; as with such guns of the era, the 7.7 cm FK 96 n.A had seats for two crewmen mounted on the splinter shield.

GWG14_491. Machine guns, mounted on mules, and their teams prepared to move out from their encampment.

GWG14_493. A platoon of Turkish troops, with their officer on the front left of the photograph.

GWG14_492. A group of Turkish officers.

GWG14_487. Officials and airmen stand by awaiting the flight of a Turkish aeroplane from St Stefano to Constantinople.

GWG14_494. Two Turkish officers in new service uniforms escort a detachment of French Moslems – captured by the Germans and thereby sent to fight for the Turks – wearing the M1909 *Kabalak* or *Enveriye* cloth helmet.

GWG14_495. Colonel Halil Bey, commander of the Constantinople garrison, is pictured on his mount.

GWG14_496. Enver Pasha – a propagandist of war. A critic of past military policy, Pasha played an instrumental role in persuading the cabinet to offer support to the Central Powers.

Chapter Six:
Seekrieg (Naval War)

'From some points of view, the German navy is to…Germany…more in the nature
of a luxury.'

In 1898, enthusiastically encouraged by the Kaiser and masterminded by Admiral von Tirpitz, the Germans passed the first of four Fleet Acts with the aim of placing the Imperial German Navy on at least fighting terms with the Royal Navy, whose ships dominated the world's oceans. Vast sums of money were spent in building up the fleet; but the British responded in kind and simply outspent and outbuilt the Germans. In 1912 the German government (secretly) abandoned the naval race, concerned that a heavy emphasis on naval expenditure had damaged the army, which had faced reduced expenditure for some years. However, this did not prevent the Germans developing strategic naval projects, most significantly the widening of the Kiel Canal (completed in June 1914), enabling dreadnought sized ships to use it, and the expansion of the German submarine fleet.

Although war had not officially broken out, a German mine off Cuxhaven sank the merchant ship *San Wilfrido* on 3 August. The *Goeben* and *Breslau*, en route to Istanbul, shelled French ports in Algeria on 4 August and soon afterwards British ships of the Grand Fleet ambushed German destroyers that had ventured out of port. The Battle of Heligoland Bight on 28 August saw a significant reverse for the Germans in the first major naval engagement of the war, costing the Imperial German Navy three light cruisers, a destroyer and the lives of 700 sailors, with some 900 other casualties at minimal cost to the British.

Elsewhere, German cruisers engaged in some notable raids: the chief of these was the Battle of the Coronel Sea off the coast of Chile on 1 November. The Royal Navy lost *Monmouth* and *Good Hope*, cruisers that were outgunned and outranged by ships of Admiral Graf Spee's squadron and the first significant British naval reverse for a century. The German triumph was, however, short lived: as a consequence of the Battle of the Falkland Islands on 8 December, von Spee's squadron was destroyed and, in effect, Germany's Blue Water surface navy had been put out of action permanently.

On 26 August the German light cruiser SMS *Magdeburg* ran aground in heavy fog off the coast of Finland. Unable to float her, the crew scuttled her when it became clear that Russian naval vessels were closing in. Of itself not particularly significant, Russian divers recovered her code books, which were passed on to the British and proved to be most useful in the early months of the North Sea naval campaign.

Most controversially, a German squadron under Admiral von Hipper shelled the English North Sea ports of Hartlepool, West Hartlepool, Whitby and Scarborough, resulting in the deaths of 137 and wounding of 592, almost all civilians. The Germans claimed that it was a legitimate naval operation, as both Hartlepool and Scunthorpe were used by the Royal Navy; however, it was something of a propaganda disaster.

The one bright hope for the German navy lay in the potential of its submarine force. Submarines were controversial; many officers of the surface fleets were far from convinced that they were civilized weapons of war and nor were they convinced of their effectiveness. Such doubts seemed to have been vindicated by the early poor results of U-boat operations. Germany had twenty submarines at the outbreak of the war, part of the High Seas Fleet and operating from bases on Heligoland. There was no unrestricted submarine warfare at this stage in the war, as the German government was concerned as to the impact this might have on neutral powers, above all to the United States. Barbara Tuchman considered that the fear was groundless, writing that 'the mass of Americans, who never saw a seacoast, could not be worked into a war fever...nor aroused to a fighting mood'.

About half of the submarine force was out on a screening patrol at the outbreak of war. Some of these were redeployed to attack the Grand Fleet at Scapa Flow; however, two (U-5 and U-9) had to turn back because of engine problems, U-13 was lost without trace, and HMS *Birmingham* sank U-15. Four other boats so engaged achieved no success. The disdain of senior commanders seemed to have been justified by this lack of worthwhile results.

However, September provided some better news for the supporter of the undersea weapon. On 5 September U-21 (Kapitänleutnant Otto Hersing) torpedoed the British light cruiser HMS *Pathfinder* off the Firth of Forth. The cruiser sank within minutes, resulting in very high casualties. On 22 September, U-9 (Kapitänleutnant Otto Weddigen) sank three cruisers in just seventy five minutes: the HMS *Aboukir*, *Hogue* and *Cressy*, with 1,460 British sailors losing their lives.

Three weeks later U-26 sank the Russian cruiser *Pallada* in the Gulf of Finland. On the same day, U-9 struck again, sinking the light cruiser HMS *Hawke* of the coast of Aberdeen. The last operation of 1914 involved U-17, which claimed the dubious distinction of being the first submarine to sink an unarmed merchant vessel, sinking the SS *Glitra*, a British merchant ship, off the south coast of Norway.

The British declared the whole of the North Sea a military zone in November (i.e. it was policed by the Royal Navy and all merchant shipping was subject to its inspection). The German High Seas Fleet had, effectively, been bottled up in its harbours, although there were the occasional forays and one large scale sortie, leading to the Battle of Jutland in May 1916. It was the submarine that was to emerge as Germany's principal naval weapon, something that was made possible largely by the capture of Belgian ports. The naval war became one of developing submarine and anti-submarine tactics. The German underseas blockade of the UK came close to success; but it did not have the same impact as the very effective British blockade of Germany, a direct cause, for example, of the so-called Turnip Winter of 1916.

GWG14_497. Loading at Zeebrugge: two German destroyers berthed adjacent to one another, load mines preparatory to a North Sea rendezvous with German submarines and mine layers.

GWG14_498. A neutral Swedish sailing barge is pictured sinking, struck by a German torpedo.

GWG14_499. Admiral Franz von Hipper architect of the German naval raid on Scarborough, December 1914.

GWG14_500. Kiel Harbour – headquarters of the German Navy, incorporating the Imperial shipbuilding yards, slips, dry and wet docks.

GWG14_501. The men who sank three British cruisers in an hour (the *Hogue*, *Aboukir* and *Cressy*): a German picture postcard bears the caption 'Our Heroes!' with the crew of submarine SM U-9 commanded by Kapitänleutnant Otto Weddigen (centre of the first row standing).

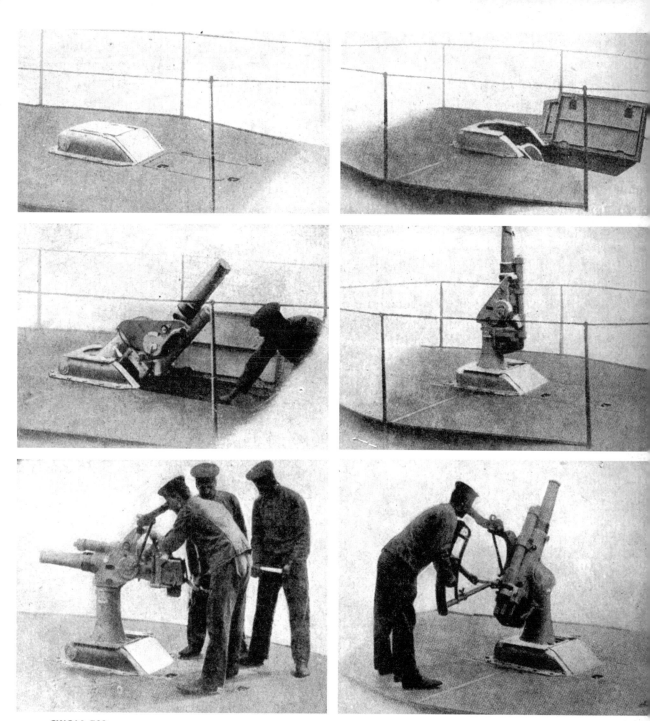

GWG14_503. On a German submarine: a 3.7 cm gun fitted on a fixed pivot mounting and carried on top of the fixed mounting in a cylindrical cradle. This defensive weapon slides backwards and forwards when in action.

GWG14_504. SM U-28 holds up a Dutch Liner, *Battavier 5*, in the North Sea. The ship was subsequently seized as a prize and escorted to Zeebrugge.

GWG14_507. The *Scharnhorst* and *Gneisenau* (pictured at the furthest fringe of the photograph on the left) depart the port of Valparaiso.

GWG14_502. The torpedo room of a 1914 German submarine. At the extreme end are three torpedoes ready for launching.

GWG14_506. A German warship is pictured coaling (restocking coal supplies) at sea.

GWG14_505. The interior of a German submarine's Control Room: the commander is pictured looking through a periscope.

GWG14_508. Following the successful destruction of the wireless station on Cocos-Keeling Island, a German landing party embarks to return to the light cruiser *Emden*.

GWG14_509. HMS *Pegasus*, which had returned to post in Zanzibar with boiler and engine problems, was sunk by a German light cruiser in September 1914.

GWG14_510. The *Goeben* flying the Turkish flag.

GWG14_511. HMS *Hawke*, a 7,000-ton light cruiser, sunk by the German submarine SM U-9 (commanded by Kapitänleutnant Otto Weddigen) off the coast of Aberdeen.

GWG14_512. Scarborough: No. 2, Wykeham Street. Four people were killed at this address.

GWG14_513. West Hartlepool: Nos. 20 and 21, Cleveland Road. Structural damage is evident, following naval incursions carried out on 16 December by the First High Seas Fleet Scouting Group, commanded by Admiral Franz von Hipper.

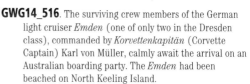

GWG14_516. The surviving crew members of the German light cruiser *Emden* (one of only two in the Dresden class), commanded by *Korvettenkapitän* (Corvette Captain) Karl von Müller, calmly await the arrival on an Australian boarding party. The *Emden* had been beached on North Keeling Island.

GWG14_517. The battered hulk of the *Emden* lies aground (far right), driven ashore and destroyed by the Australian cruiser HMS *Sydney*.

GWG14_514. Sunk without warning: taken from the deck of a U-boat (foreground), a tramp steamer pictured in the distance erupts into flame, a torpedo having struck her hull. International law permitted the destruction of merchant shipping only if the crew could be saved.

GWG14_515. The officers of a German submarine, having surfaced during daylight hours, are pictured atop the conning tower.

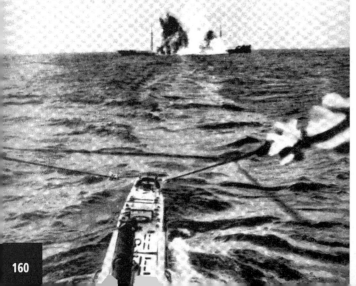

GWG14_518. The German battle cruiser *Goeben*, assigned to the Ottoman Fleet, August 1914; she was subsequently renamed *Yavuz Sultan Selim*.

GWG14_519. German submarine SM U-15 sunk – rammed – by HMS *Birmingham* off Fair Isle, 9 August. This was the first U-boat to be lost to enemy action; all hands were lost.

GWG14_520. The *Ophelia*, a German hospital ship, is escorted to port by a British torpedo boat (far right, silhouetted against the backdrop) in the North Sea, having suffered the loss of all wireless function, dismantled by the British boarding party.

GWG14_521. German naval officers in their wardroom.

GWG14_522. Substatial weapons: two of the eight 8.2inch guns carried by the *Scharnhorst*, which was a successful raider in the early months of the war, before she was sunk with the loss of all hands.

GWG14_523. German naval petty officers following the completion of a training course.

GWG14_525. *Überzieher* (Bluejackets) of the German armoured cruiser *Scharnhorst* stand aboard a small steamer ship in their working rig.

GWG14_524. The *Kronprinzessin Cecilie* (Crown Princess Cecilie), the famous 'Gold Ship'. On 28 July 1914 the liner departed New York for Bremen, its home port, carrying a consignment of gold and silver valued at some $3 million and over 1,200 passengers, with its first port of call Liverpool. At the outbreak of war it was instructed to head for the neutral USA; where it was, eventually, seized and the gold and passengers transferred off.

GWG14_526. An armed cruiser submarine tender, tasked with replenishing U-boats at sea. The armed personnel on the port bow are preparing to disembark and board the Dutch steamer *Zannstroom*.

Chapter Seven:
Die Heimatfront (The Home Front)

'The war rent asunder the traditional German 'home'. Millions of husbands and fathers were absent at the front while hundreds of thousands of women worked in industrial plants.'

The reaction to the outbreak of war in Germany was broadly similar to that in the capitals of the other countries that were engaged in the conflict: general enthusiasm on the streets, general support for the war in the various parliaments and their equivalents, muted opposition generally only coming from some branches of the socialist and trade union movements, an opposition which existed to a greater or lesser extent in all of the combatant nations.

In the first weeks of the war the press engaged in almost unanimous support of the conflict, portraying Germany as being the victim of conspiring European powers (possibly none more hated than 'perfidious Albion') and that the German people were engaged in a quasi religious mission: the 'August experience' was a 'holy flame of anger', a 'revelation' and assuredly 'the holy hour' had come. Soldiers entraining for the front were bedecked with flowers and had treats and chocolate pressed on them. A simply staggering 1,500,000 verses and poems were reported to have been composed in support of the war or of the fighting German men – about an average of 50,000 a day. The war was portrayed – and seen – as an essential measure to ensure the safeguarding of the Reich and the Fatherland.

Although there was an enthusiastic response to the mobilization of reserves, there was no need for the sort of response that was necessary in Britain to the call of Lord Kitchener and others for volunteers. Volunteers there certainly were (most famously, perhaps, one Adolf Hitler, who got special permission to enlist into the Bavarian army), but Prussia and other semi-independent armies within the German Empire – as indeed was the case for France – had a well developed and well planned system of mobilizing her forces on the basis of her system of conscription.

To the untutored public all seemed to be going well in the war in the first weeks, with the exception of the scare of early Russian successes in East Prussia. This was a particularly sensitive area, as East Prussia was in many ways the spiritual home of the Hohenzollern dynasty and by extension of the Empire – after all, this was the stamping ground of the Teutonic Knights. Not for nothing was the five day battle at the very end of August that restored the situation and repelled the Russian savages given the topographically misleading name of Tannenberg.

However, short war as it was expected to be, people high and low did their bit for the war effort. Great houses and chateaux were dedicated to the wounded – for example, the widow of the Archduke Rudolf converted a castle into a 200 bed hospital; whilst Katharina Schratt, the Emperor Franz Josef's long term 'companion' offered her Viennese mansion for a similar purpose. There was much handing over of jewelry and rings to be melted down to help finance the war. In both German and Austrian society women set up sewing and knitting circles to provide warm clothes and other comforts for the troops; whilst municipalities also conducted fund raisers and similar activities to support their men at the front – for example, the collecting of books for field libraries was a popular charity.

However, by the end of the year it was quite clear that this was not going to be as short a war as everyone had hoped. Previous experience of European wars in the late nineteenth century had all indicated that wars were short and sharp; this one was proving to be very different. Certain straight forward measures had already been imposed – for example censorship of the press. It became apparent that, in the light of the British blockade, action would need to be taken to make the most of raw materials that had originally been supplied either exclusively or principally from abroad. There were soon issues regarding the supply of food – surprisingly, perhaps, the Germans were rather ineffective at organizing a coherent and effective system of food distribution and rationing for civilians – although in these early months this was not a major issue. Nevertheless, it has to be said that there was no planned stockpiling and even the forces in the field often had to operate under the traditional system of living off the land – a policy that proved to be particularly damaging to the cavalry.

Thus, at Christmas 1914, 'for the soldiers of the home front…there was but one thought: victory in 1915'.

GWG14_527. Augusta Victoria, Empress of Germany, at a railway station in Berlin, taking leave of nurses organized by the Order of Johanita, the Prussian Protestant successor to the Knights of Malta.

GWG14_528. Shell casings were carefully collected by both sides after use for recycling: here a French farmer is engaged in loading a dump of them onto a wagon.

GWG14_529. Wounded and recuperating German soldiers out for a walk with a nurse in Berlin.

GWG14_530. Like her sister the Duchess of Westminster, the Princess of Pless nurses wounded servicemen in Germany.

GWG14_532. A wounded soldier is conveyed across the streets of Berlin by members of the 'Paramedics Berlin Bicycle Club', using a dual-purpose bicycle-cart.

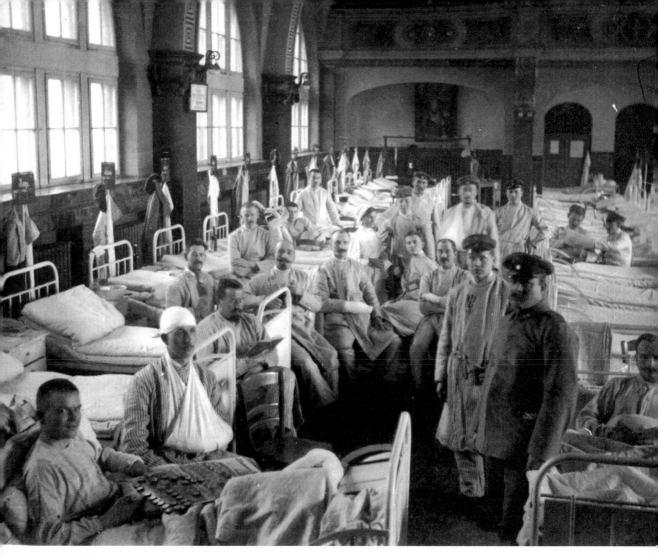

GWG14_533. German wounded in a military hospital back home in Germany.

GWG14_534. Mounds of bedding are loaded onto wagon-carts in Vienna to be transported to the front for use by the Austrian Army in the field.

GWG14_538. An officer of the German army reads out the declaration of war to an attentive crowd in Berlin.

GWG14_539. A family portrait: father and son sit proudly for the camera. The son (right) is an officer cadet in Foot Guards Infanterie-Regiment Nr. 3; the father a major in the German army. Both wear the 'Swedish Cuff' (a horizontal panel around the circumference of the cuff, with two buttons evenly spaced) worn exclusively by members of the Foot Guards Infanterie-Regiments, Nr. 1 – 4.

GWG14_542. A German soldier off to war waits while a bouquet of flowers is pinne his breast tunic by a lady admirer – possibly his sweetheart

GWG14_541. A troop of Marine Reservists stands on a station platform in Germany awaiting a train to the docks.

GWG14_543. A German soldier assists one of his comrades with adjusting his kit, part of a group of troops preparing to move off to the front from their depot at home.

GWG14_544. A woman hands flowers to a German soldier on his way to the railway station.

GWG14_545. Mobilized Austro-Hungarian troops talk with friends and relatives who are pressed against the barrack's gates.

GWG14_546. Three members of a quartermaster's staff play Skat in their stores.

GWG14_547. *Tee-Bombe*, a simple solution to the problems of war: 'an aromatic, golden clear advert for tea'.

Die „**Tee-Bombe**" ergibt durch einfaches Schwenken in siedendem Wasser **im Nu eine Literportion** köstlichen, aromatischen, goldklaren und gesüßten Tee („Marke Teekanne") für 10 Pfennige! Ueberall erhältlich, sonst Bezugsquellennachweis durch **R. Seelig & Hille, Dresden 214.**

GWG14_548. The product of a food drive in aid of the German war effort is sorted, packaged and prepared for transportation to the front.

GWG14_549. Reading drive: books bought using money donated by German citizens are sorted and boxed ready for shipping to German troops at the front.

GWG14_552. A recreation of a French fortification, made almost entirely from wool, in a German ministry building.

GWG14_550. A 'soldier' of the German army accompanies a district postman – employed in Berlin – on his rounds.

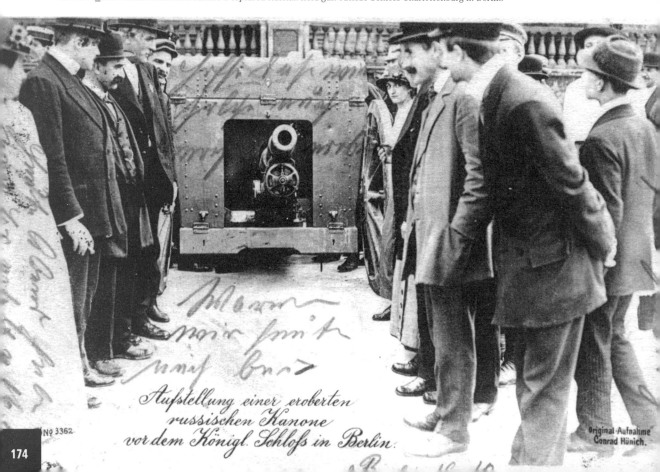

GWG14_551. German 'soldiers' collect money, as part of a drive in support of the German war effort; one child (centre) wears a Red Cross brassard.

GWG14_553. Local inhabitants admire a captured Russian field gun outside Schloss Charlottenburg in Berlin.

Russische Maschinengewehre er der Kommandatur in Berlin.

rginalaufnahme vom Kriegsschauplatz
Im Schützengraben.

GWG14_554. *Russische Maschinengewehre* (PM M1910), seized during the advance across the Eastern Front, are exhibited in the garden of the commandant of Berlin.

GWG14_555. Greetings from the Eastern Front: a picture postcard originally colourised captures a troop of German infantry in *schützengraben* (a trench) in East Prussia.

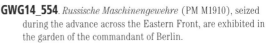

Verlustlisten

GWG14_558. *Verlustlitsen* (casualty lists) posted publically for German civilians – in this case Berliners – to see. Similar scenes took place in the capitals of other combatant capitals, such as London and Paris.

Nur immer langsam, Jhr kommt ja alle dran!

GWG14_557. Members of the Landwehr-Infanterie-Regiment Nr. 73 distribute aid to Belgian civilians.

GWG14_556. 'Just wait, patiently, you will all get your turn,' reads a German picture postcard.

Timeline 1914

28 June The Archduke Franz Ferdinand assassinated in the Bosnian capital, Sarajevo.

23 July Austro-Hungarian ultimatum delivered to Serbian assembly.

28 July Austria-Hungary declares war on Serbia.

29 July Austrian forces bombard Belgrade. Germany refuses to adhere to Belgian neutrality. Secret alliance signed between Turkey and Germany in Berlin.

30 July Germany sends Russia written notification warning that partial mobilization will result in a state of war. Austro-Hungarian General Staff issue orders for the mobilization of all Austrian forces.

31 July Russia orders general mobilization of all forces.

1 August German High Command orders general mobilization at 5pm. A declaration of war is sent to Russia two hours later.

2 August Germany invades Luxembourg and demands permission from neutral Belgium to allow German forces to move through that country – which is refused on the 3rd. Russian Poland invaded by Germany; Kalish, Chenstokhov and Bendzin are overrun the following day. The German light cruisers, *Augsburg* and *Magdeburg*, bombards Libau, a Baltic Province of Latvia (Russia).

3 August Germany declares war on France and begins implementing a modified form of the Schlieffen Plan, crossing into Belgium. A German mine laid off Cuxhaven sinks the SS *San Wilfrido*.

4 August Germany declares war on Belgium. Great Britain declares war on Germany at 11pm British time. Battle and Siege of Liége commences; six brigades of the German *Second Army* attempt to storm the forts of the historic city. Only one brigade is successful; the city holds out. German siege artillery proceeds thereafter to bombard the remaining forts. German warships *Goeben* and *Breslau* bombard Philippeville and Bona respectively.

6 August Austria-Hungary declares war on Russia. Fighting erupts in Soldau, East Prussia, between Russian and German cavalry.

7 August German forces occupy the city of Liége but some forts still hold out.

8 August Wireless tower and station, Dar-es-Salaam, German East Africa, shelled by British light cruisers *Astraea* and *Pegasus*. The industrial city of Mulhouse is occupied by the French Army during the Battle of Mulhouse; they are partially ejected on the 11th.

12 August Russian forces invade East Prussia, advancing towards Stallupönen and Gumbinnen. In Sabac, Serbia, Austrian troops execute Serbian civilians. Great Britain and France declare war on Austria-Hungary. The Battle of Haelen begins: Belgian troopers at the bridge of Haelen waylay German cavalry attempting to cross.

13 August Austrian Fifth and Sixth Armies cross the River Drina, heralding the first invasion of Serbia.

14 August Battle of Morhange-Sarrebourg: French First and Second Armies cross the Franco-German border. The German counter-attack exacts a heavy toll; French casualties are high.

16 August German forces end the Siege of Liege, capturing the remaining forts. Light cruiser *Zenta* is sunk off the coast of Montenegro with fifty killed and wounded.

17 August General Hermann von Francois, I Corps Commander, instigates first major offensive of the Eastern Front at Stallupönen; 3,000 Russian soldiers are captured.

20 August Battle of Gumbinnen: German *Seventh Army* launches a hesitant attack northward across a 55km front; the offensive is routed, prompting a general retreat to the Vistula. The Battle of Morhange-Sarrebourg ends, German *Sixth Army* having counterattacked occupying the town of Morhange.

21 August The French Fifth Army encounters the German *Second* and *Third Armies* at the Battle of Charleroi: the French cannot hold and a general retreat is ordered. The numerically superior German *Fourth* and *Fifth Armies* halt the French advance in the Ardennes region at the Battle of the Ardennes.

22 August In under a day, the French army loses 27,000 men killed during the abortive Battles of the Frontiers.

23–24 August Battle of Mons, the first encounter between British and German troops on the Western front. The German *First Army* forced the withdrawal of the BEF's four British Infantry divisions; 'The Retreat from Mons' begins. Japan declares war on Germany. French Fifth Army withdraws from the mid-size industrial town of Charleroi, ending the Battle of Charleroi.

24 August French forces in the Ardennes begin an orderly retreat toward Verdun, pursued by the German *Third Army*; the Battle of the Ardennes is over.

25 August The German *Seventh Army* completes the recapture of Mulhouse, ending the Battle of Mulhouse. The Battle of Lorraine ends. German gains are minimal, limited to a small salient in French lines.

26 August Battle of Tannenburg, in East Prussia – Russians evacuate newly-captured Allenstein, creating a vulnerable salient in the line. At the Battle of Le Cateau, the German *First Army* forces the withdrawal of the British Expeditionary Force: British casualties are high, mainly prisoners: 865 killed. SMS *Magdeburg* runs aground in heavy fog off the coast of Finland and is scuttled by the crew. French Fourth Army waylays the German *Fourth* and *Fifth Armies* at the Battle of the Meuse.

27 August Austrian *Fourth Army* in Russian Poland takes Zamosc, capturing about 20,000 Russian troops; Cossack forces, however, rout the Austrian cavalry.

28 August The First Battle of Heligoland Bight, a decisive British victory. German losses: three light cruisers, destroyer *V-187* and 700 sailors. The French Fourth Army withdraws to the towns of Verdun, Stenay and Sedan, ending the Battle of the Meuse.

29 August Joint task force, British and Indian troops combined, occupy German Samoa. In the Battle of Guise, the French Fifth Army launches a counter-attack, withdrawing late in the afternoon. Russian First and Second Armies retire from East Prussia, ending the Russian invasion and the Battle of Tannenburg. 95,000 Russian troops are captured and an estimated 30,000 killed or wounded. The Germans suffered fewer than 20,000 casualties.

30 August Austrian forces take the town of Krasnostav, 40 miles inside Poland. In Galicia, fourteen Austrian divisions are defeated on the River Gnila Lipa by twenty-two Russian divisions.

2 September Anglo-Japanese forces commence bombardment of the German held port of Tsingtao (Qingdao, China).

4 September Russian forces retreat from Mlawa, Poland, after several sustained attacks from East Prussia. The German *Sixth Army* engages the French Second Army at the Battle of Grand Couronné, but fail to capture the prize, the city of Nancy.

5 September U-21 sank the light British cruiser, HMS *Pathfinder*, off the Firth of Forth.

6 September The German *First Army* advance's toward the French capital is halted at the Ourcq River during the First Battle of the Marne.

7 September German naval squadron severs the British Pacific communications cable.

9 September The German *Eighth Army* at the Battle of Masurian Lakes accosts two divisions of the Russian Second Army, covering the ordered retreat of their comrades across east Prussia.

11 September The Australian Naval and Military Expeditionary Force (AN&MEF) lands at the island of Neupommern, German New Guinea.

12 September The exposed right flank of the German *First Army* is assaulted by elements of the French Fifth Army during the First Battle of the Aisne. The first Battle of the Marne ends with the German I Army in retreat; it is a victory for the allies. The German attack on Nancy collapses. The German *Sixth Army* retires, ending the Battle of Grand Couronné.

14 September Russian retreat across East Prussia is concluded at the Battle of the Masurian Lakes. An expedient withdrawal, though ordered, proves costly: 125,000 Russian soldiers are lost.

15 September First Battle of the Aisne is concluded, Allied forces make few gains and trench warfare is said to have commenced. Instead, both parties attempt to manoeuvre northward towards the open flack, each intending to outrace the other.

17 September The Island of Neupommern is liberated by Australian troops.

22 September U-9 sinks three cruisers: HMS *Aboukir*, *Hogue* and *Cressy*, off the Hook of Holland.

25 September The First Battle of Albert: the German *Sixth Army* halts the advance of General De Castenau's Second Army along the entire front, Oise to the Somme.

26 September The Wireless station at Anguar on the Palau Islands is assaulted by AN&MEF.

28 September Siege of Antwerp: heavy German siege artillery shells Antwerp's outlying ring of forts.

29 September French Second Army forced to retire north of Albert due to heavy German resistance, ending the First Battle of Albert.

1 October The First Battle of Arras: primarily a mistake by the German Army in early September. Three corps of the German *First*, *Second* and *Seventh Armies* mount an attack on the town.

4 October A sustained and aggressive onslaught by German *First*, *Second* and *Seventh Armies* threatens to encircle Arras. The French Tenth Army holds out, bringing to a close the First Battle of Arras.

7 October The order to evacuate the city of Antwerp is given and the German army occupies the city by nightfall.

9 October German seamen land at Mtao, where, by employing explosive charges, they sink the *Del Commune*.

11 October U-26 sinks the Russian cruiser *Pallada* in the Gulf of Finland and SM U-9 sinks the light cruiser HMS *Hawke* off Aberdeen.

18 October Battle of the Yser: the German Fourth Army launches an against Belgian forces deployed east of the Yser canal.

19 October First Battle of Ypres begins. The German *Fourth Army* over the next four weeks engages the BEF's I Corps.

20 October U-17 sinks the British steamer SS *Glitra*, a precursor of several later events. SS *Glitra* was the first merchant vessel sunk by a submarine.

28 October Ottoman naval craft bombard Russian held fishing ports in the Black Sea. The Ottoman Empire enters the war on the side of the Central Powers.

29 October The German *Fourth Army* is forced to a standstill at the Battle of the Yser, the Belgians having flooded the low lying countryside.

1 November Russia declares war on the Ottoman Empire. Bergmann Offensive launched, Russian forces cross the Russo-Turkish divide. The Turkish *Third Army's* counter-attack forces the withdrawal of Russian troops. The British Navy suffers its worst reverse in a hundred years: the *Monmouth* and *Good Hope* are sunk.

4 November Allied powers declare war on the Ottoman Empire.

6 November British forces land at Shatt al-Arab and advance south toward the Turkish fort of Fao (Al-Faw). German authorities on the isle of Nauru surrender to a detachment of fifty soldiers under the command of Colonel Holmes.

7 November German troops at the port of Tsingtao surrender to Anglo-Japanese forces. Ottoman troops respond to Russian advances in the Caucasus. The Turkish *Third Army* and *XI Corps* advance and later retreat, though holding ground at Köprüköy. The Austrian *Fifth* and *Sixth Armies* cross the Drina, forcing the Serbian defenders to withdraw to the Jadar road.

8 November Austro-Hungarian troops enter Valjevo. British forces successfully capture the Turkish fortress of Fao.

11 November British and Indian forces confront the Turks on the outskirts of Basra. 1,200 Arab conscripts are captured.

16 November Austrian troops reach the Kolubara.

19 November The German *Ninth Army*, aiding beleaguered Austrian forces, confront the Russian First and Second Armies at the Battle of Lodz.

22 November The onset of winter and the exhaustion of men and materiel brings the first Battle of Ypres to a close and the end of major operations for the year on the Western Front.

25 November The German *Ninth Army* is victorious at the Battle of Lodz; Russian First Army is rendered ineffective and Second Army is forced to retire 70 miles, ending the Russian occupation of East Prussia.

1 December The Austrian Army captures Belgrade.

8 December The Battle of the Falkland Islands: Royal Navy warships destroy the German squadron of Admiral Graf von Spee off the coast of Argentina.

10 December Serbian forces retake the Drina River.

13 December British submarine, HMS *B11*, sinks *Mesûdiye*, the Ottoman Navy's sole coastal defence craft.

15 December Serbian troops reoccupy the city of Belgrade; Austro-Hungarian forces are in retreat.

16 December First High Seas Fleet Scouting Group bombards the North Sea English seaports of Hartlepool, West Hartlepool, Whitby and Scarborough; 137 are killed and 592 wounded.

18 December Attacking British troops at Givenchy encounter a solidly entrenched German force around the village.

20 December First Battle of Champagne, the first major offensive against the German line, begins. The French make minor territorial gains across the line. French and German casualties number some 90,000 each.

21 December The end of the Defence of Givenchy: British casualties are high, at 4,000, double those of the Germans.

21 December Jasin (East Africa) occupied by British forces.

26 December A mine, laid off the Bosphorus, damages SMS *Goeben*.

29 December Turkish 30th Division attacks Alisofu; three Russian battalions rout the Turkish troops. The Battle of Sarıkamış begins.

Bibliography

Barker, A.J. *The First Iraq War, 1914–1918: Britain's Mesopotamian Campaign*. Enigma Books, 2009.

Beatty, J. *The Lost History of 1914: Reconsidering the Year the Great War Began*. Walker & Company, 2012.

Bloom, H. *Erich Maria Remarque's All Quiet on the Western Front*. Vintage, 2009.

Bilton, D. *The Germans at Arras*. Pen & Sword, 2009.

Bilton, D. *The Central Powers on the Russian Front, 1914–1918*. Pen & Sword, 2014.

Cashman, G. *An Introduction to the Causes of War: Patterns of Interstate Conflict from World War One to Iraq*. Rowmand & Littlefield Publishers, Inc, 2007.

Hans Ehlert, Michael Epkenhans, Gerhard P. Gross, David T. Zabecki eds., *The Schlieffen Plan: International Perspectives on the German Strategy for World War I*, University Press of Kentucky, 2014.

Hastings, M. *Catastrophe: Europe Goes to War 1914*. William Collins, 2013.

Herwig, H. *The First World War: Germany and Austria-Hungary, 1914–1918*. Bloomsbury Academic, 1996.

Jordan, D. *The Balkans, Italy & Africa 1914–1918: From Sarajevo to the Piave and Lake Tanganyika*. Amber Books Ltd, 2014.

Jukes, G. *The First World War: Eastern Front 1914–1918*. Osprey Publishing, 2002.

Kelly, P.J., *Tirpitz and the Imperial German Navy*. Indiana University Press, 2011.

Lucas, J.S., *Austro-Hungarian Infantry, 1914–1918*. Almark Publications, 1973.

Nash, D.B. *Imperial German Army Handbook, 1914–1918*. Ian Allan, 1980.

Philpott, W. *War of Attrition: Fighting the First World War*. Overlook Press, 2014.

Rogers, D. *Imperial German Army 1914–18*. Helion & Company, 2006.

Shankland, P. *Phantom Flotilla: Story of the Naval Africa Expedition, 1915–16*. Mayflower, 1969.

Spears, E. *Liaison 1914: A Narrative of the Great Retreat*. W&N, 2000.

Stone, N. *The Eastern Front 1914–1917*. Penguin, 1998.

Temperley, H. *England and the Near East: The Crimea*. Longman, 1936.

Traub, Gottfried, 'Heilige Gegenwart,' *Illustrierte Zeitung* (Leipzig), No.3713, 27 August 1914, p.344 – Spirit.

Verhey, J. *The Spirit of 1914: Militarism, Myth and Mobilisation in Germany*. Cambridge University Press, 2000.

von Lettow-Vorbeck, G. *My Reminiscences of East Africa*. Naval & Military Press, 2004.

Woodward, D. *Armies of the World: 1854–1914*. G.P. Putnam's Sons, 1978.